Edward W. Arms

A Genealogical Record of the Arms Family in This Country

Embracing all the known descendants of William first, who have retained

the family name, and the first generation of the descendants of other

names

Edward W. Arms

A Genealogical Record of the Arms Family in This Country
*Embracing all the known descendants of William first, who have retained the family
name, and the first generation of the descendants of other names*

ISBN/EAN: 9783337219987

Printed in Europe, USA, Canada, Australia, Japan

Cover: Foto ©ninafisch / pixelio.de

More available books at **www.hansebooks.com**

A GENEALOGICAL RECORD

OF

THE ARMS FAMILY

IN THIS COUNTRY,

EMBRACING ALL THE KNOWN DESCENDANTS OF

WILLIAM FIRST,

WHO HAVE RETAINED THE FAMILY NAME, AND THE FIRST GENERATION
OF THE DESCENDANTS OF OTHER NAMES.

BY EDWARD W. ARMS.

TROY, N. Y.:
PUBLISHED BY THE AUTHOR.
1877.

INTRODUCTION.

This work was undertaken for personal gratification, but as it grew in dimensions, there were many urgent requests to publish it, that others might be equally gratified.

That it may have errors, it would be unreasonable to deny, but the author has endeavored to carefully compile the information obtained from a voluminous correspondence, and those who assisted by sending their records will please accept his thanks, without being specified by name, for they are many. It has been suggested, that for future use it would be well to have all mistakes corrected. To that end, the author will carefully record and preserve any additions or corrections that may be sent to him from time to time.

The addition of the children of daughters of the family was an afterthought, and no special effort was made to collect such a list until quite recently.

The figures preceding parents' names indicate the page where may be found the names of their parents, and those preceding childrens' names the page of their children.

EDWARD W. ARMS.

TROY, N. Y., September 1st, 1877.

FIRST GENERATION.

WILLIAM, born 1654, died August 25th, 1731, married Joanna Hawks, 1677, who died Nov. 22, 1729.

William Arms, the ancestor of the Arms family in the United States, came from either the Island of Jersey or Guernsey, in the English Channel. It is presumed that he assumed the name of Arms, as none of this name are found on the island from whence he came. He was a knitter of stockings by trade. The first heard of him was his marriage with Joanna, daughter of John Hawks, one of the settlers of Hadley, Mass., in 1677. His name appears in the town records of Hatfield, Mass., in 1677. He removed from Hatfield to Deerfield, Mass., about 1684. It is said of him that he was a good farmer, industrious and economical, devotional and religious, and a quiet and obliging neighbor. He would knit a pair of stockings while going to and returning from the mill at Hatfield. In 1698 he was chosen farm viewer, and one of a committee to build a school house and hire a schoolmaster; in 1699, a constable; in 1700 a tythingman; in 1701, fence viewer and school commissioner. After that his name appears almost yearly in the town records. Also in the records of Sunderland, Mass., from 1714 to 1722, where he is spoken of as "Good Mr. Arms." He served in the Indian fight at Great Falls, where now is Gill, Mass., May 17, 1676, for which his son John was one of those entitled to the township granted by the General Court 1736. His body lies in the old burying ground at Deerfield, a little east of the center of the grounds, adjacent to his son William and grandson William.

SECOND GENERATION.

5 Children of **William 1st.** Deerfield, Mass.

WILLIAM, born 1678, died 1696.

7 JOHN, born 1679, died 1753, married Hannah Nash ; lived in the
third house from the south end of the main street, Deerfield, now
owned by Richard C. Arms.

SARAH, born 1681, married Jedediah Williams in 1700, who died in
Indian captivity in 1703. Afterwards married Thomas Allen, of
Northampton, Mass.

MARGARET, born 1683, married William Belding in 1700, moved to
Norwalk, Conn.

✓ 7 DANIEL, born 1686, died Sept. 28, 1753, married Esther Smead 1716.
Lived on the south-east corner of the main street, Deerfield.

EBENEZER,born 1689, died 1690 in Deerfield.

7 WILLIAM 2D, born 1692, died Sept. 27, 1774 ; married Rebecca Nash
October 28, 1720, who was burned to death in his house May 12,
1768. Lived on the south-west corner of the main street, Deerfield. He was a devout and sincere christian—a strict Puritan. He
and his wife were admitted to full communion with the church un-
der Rev. Jonathan Ashley in 1736. His profession, farming. He
was a peaceful and inoffensive neighbor. Buried between his
father and son in the old Deerfield burying ground.

ELIZABETH, born 1695, died Oct. 1, 1772, married Ebenezer Field,
who was killed accidentally Sept. 12, 1726. Afterwards married
Azariah Wright, 1726. She was the first schooldame in Northfield,
and a noted woman there.

THIRD GENERATION.

6 Children of **John,** son of William 1st, Deerfield.

HANNAH,•born 1713, died 1751 ; married John Hinsdale.

NANCY, (by some called Mercy,) born 1718 ; married John Sheldon.

8 JOHN (Major John), born 1722, died 1763, married Susannah Willard. The Major was one of the first settlers at Fort Dummer (now called Dummer Meadows), Brattleboro, the first civilized establishment in the present limits of Vermont. He kept a noted inn there, and was killed by a kick from a horse.

6 Children of **Daniel,** son of William 1st, Deerfield.

SUBMIT, born 1718, died 1718.

8 DANIEL, 2d, b. 1719, d. May 4. 1784, married Mary Stebbins, d. 1798.

8 EBENEZER, b. Jan. 29, 1721, d. March 12, 1789, married Elizabeth Allen, Jan. 25, 1747 ; residence Greenfield, Mass.

MOSES, born 1722, died 1733.

. ESTHER, born 1723, married John Severance.

AARON, born 1725, died 1735.

MARTHA, born 1728, married Othniel Taylor.

ABNER, born 1731.

MOSES, born 1733, died 1733.

SETH, born 1734, died 1736.

8 CONSIDER, born Oct. 15, 1736, died June 19, 1792, married Mary Catlin, Dec. 10, 1765. She died Feb. 12, 1822.

6 Children of **William 2d,** son of William 1st, Deerfield.

REBECCA, born 1722, married David Childs and Nathaniel Phelps.

9 WILLIAM, 3d, born June 25, 1724, died May, 1794, married Elizabeth Belding, who died Feb. 24, 1804, residence Deerfield. He was reputed an honest, prudent and industrious farmer of great enterprise. He lies buried near his father. Inscription on stone, "An honest man the noblest work of God."

9 ELIJAH, born 1724, married Experience Hawks, South Deerfield.

9 THOMAS, born 1729, married Lydia Alvord, South Deerfield.

PHINEAS, b. 1731, d. 1755, killed by Indians at Charlemont, Mass.

10 JONATHAN, born Jan. 27, 1735 (n. s.) died Feb. 13, 1819, married Rebecca Hinsdale July 3d, 1760, who died Nov. 16, 1773 ; married Eunice Lyman Dec. 6, 1774, who died May 3, 1838. Deerfield.

10 DAVID, born Jan. 27, 1735, (twin brother of Jonathan) died at Canaan, N. Y.

10 ELIAKIM, b. 1737, d. 1810, married Esther Bridgeman, So. Deerfield.

FOURTH GENERATION.

7 Children of **Major John,** son of John. Brattleboro, Vt.

WILLARD, born 1744, died 1751.

SUSANNAH, born 1747, married —— Willard.

11 JOSIAH, born March 17, 1750, at Deerfield ; died 1803 at Brattleboro, Vt.; married Cynthia Avery. His inn was the headquarters of many of the officers of the State government, and as such was once attacked by a party of Yorkers, Jan. 17, 1784.

HANNAH, born 1753.

LUCINDA, born 1757, married Dr. Dickerman.

JOHN WILLARD, born 1759, died 1783.

7 Children of **Daniel 2d,** son of Daniel 1st.

SUBMIT, born 1744, died 1744.

MARY, born 1747, married Simeon Harvey.

11 AARON, born 1749, married 1806, married Lucy Tyler.

ESTHER, born 1754, married Thomas Migbells.

MARTHA, born 1762, married Zur Hawks.

EXPERIENCE, born 1777, married Peter Gates.

7 Children of **Ebenezer,** son of Daniel 1st. Greenfield, Mass.

MARY, born March 25, 1748. Greenfield.

11 MOSES, born Oct. 12, 1749, died aged 68 years. Greenfield.

EBENEZER, born Nov. 28, 1751, died Sept. 8, 1758. Greenfield.

GRACE, born Sept. 12, 1753. Greenfield.

ELIZABETH, born Aug. 16, 1755, married John Newton. Greenfield.

12 EBENEZER, born April, 1760, died July 6, 1812 ; married Mary White, who died Dec. 26, 1837. She was a descendant of the Mrs. White who was the first person to step ashore from the " Mayflower" on American soil.

12 JESSE, born August 2, 1771, at Greenfield ; died May 16, 1820 ; he moved to Duxbury, Vt., in 1795 ; married Lucretia Craig 1797, who died June 26, 1805.

7 Children of **Consider,** son of Daniel 1st. Conway, Mass.

12 DANIEL, born July 23, 1766, died Nov. 11, 1830; married Luany Crosby Aug. 11, 1792, who died July, 1809 ; then married Nancy Thompson, Jan. 26, 1814. Sodus, N. Y.

ISRAEL, born Oct. 24, 1767, died Sept. 25, 1795.

13 HENRY, born July 10, 1769, died May 7, 1848 ; married Experience Gates Jan. 31, 1798, who died Dec. 30, 1848. Conway, Mass.

SOPHIA, born Dec. 1, 1770, married April, 1791.

DOROTHY, born Oct. 31, 1772, married Jan. 10, 1792.

13 JOHN, born Feb. 26, 1774, died June, 1856 ; married Martha Bolt-
wood, Jan. 23, 1800. Conway, Mass.

POLLY, born Nov. 17, 1775, married Feb. 10, 1799.

MERCY, born Dec. 1, 1776.

14 CHRISTOPHER, born Oct. 7, 1777, died May, 1855 ; married Fanny
Allen, 1803, died Sept. 14, 1810, and Paulina Clary. Conway, Mass.

LOUISA, born June 17, 1779, died August 30, 1782.

14 OLIVER, born June 26, 1780, married 1822.

14 ABNER, born Aug. 16, 1781, died Nov. 1845 ; married Electa Boyden, Jan. 1, 1812 ; she died July, 1854, in Philadelphia ; he died in
North Carolina.

LOUISA, born Dec. 18, 1783, married Oct. 1808.

CLARISSA, born Dec. 17, 1786, married July, 1812.

7 Children of **William 3d,** son of William 2d. Deerfield.

ELIZABETH, born 1750, died Feb. 24, 1815, at Croyden, N. H.

NOAH, born 1753, died 1756.

PHINEAS, born 1756, died 1757.

14 PHINEAS, born 1759, died Oct. 10, 1838 ; married Lydia Root. Mont
Rose, N. Y.

SUBMIT, born 1760, married Consider Scott.

35 JOANNA, born 1762, died April 13, 1813, at Newport, N. H.; married Daniel Chapin.

35 ASENATH, born 1764, died Dec. 5, 1822, at Croyden, N. H. ; married Rev. Jacob Havens.

35 HULDAH, born 1766, married Amos Fisher.

14 WILLIAM 4th, born Dec. 8, 1769, died Sept. 27, 1813. He inherited
the homestead, and married Mercy Snow, daughter of Capt. Samuel Snow, of Goshen, Mass. ; she died July 17, 1817. He studied
law with Mr. Sargeant, of Windsor, Conn., practiced for a time in
Simsbury, and afterwards removed to Plainfield, N. H. He lost
his property in an unfortunate patent right speculation, and died at
Painted Post, N. Y.

7 Children of **Elijah,** son of William 2d. South Deerfield.

15 ELIJAH, JR., born 1760, married Esther Lyman. South Deerfield.

ELECTA, born 1763, married Seth Nims. North Deerfield.

EXPERIENCE, born 1770, married Solomon Graves.

7 Children of **Thomas,** son of William 2d. Deerfield.

15 ELIPHAS, born 1754, married Miriam Wright. South Deerfield.

16 SETH, born July 1, 1757, married Joanna Wright, March, 1781. Bernardston, Mass.

16 THOMAS, JR., born Aug. 3, 1759, died June 2, 1832 ; married Polly
Coolridge, died June, 1794, married Hannah Boyden, Oct. 1795.

2

LYDIA, born 1762, married Josiah Haddock.

JOSIAH, born April 12, 1764.

CLARISSA, born 1766.

16 RUFUS, born April 12, 1768, married Sarah Halbert.

16 LEMUEL, born Nov. 27, 1769, married Sarah Anderson, 1790. South Deerfield.

LUCY, born 1774.

7 Children of **Deacon Jonathan**, son of William 2d. Deerfield.

REBECCA, born 1761, married Edward Billings.

MIRANDA, born 1764, married Solomon Williams. Deerfield.

16 JONATHAN, JR., born 1766, married Sarah Wells. Montpelier, Vt.

SOPHIA, b. 1769, married Deacon Cotton Partridge. Hatfield, Mass.

MIRIAM, born 1771, died 1794.

LUCINDA, born 1773, died 1783.

EUNICE, born 1775, married Augustus Lyman.

16 PLINY, born Feb. 17, 1778, died at Deerfield, Feb. 2, 1859, married Thankful Dickinson June 19, 1810.

DOROTHY, born 1779, died 1779.

17 GEORGE, born 1780, died Oct. 31, 1819, at Deerfield ; married Fanny Cushing.

DOROTHY, born 1783, died Aug. 20, 1852, at Deerfield ; married Jacob Smith.

17 JOSIAH LYMAN, born May 25, 1788, died Dec. 12, 1828, at Glens Falls, N. Y. ; married Cynthia G. Hunt, Oct. 15, 1812, who died Dec. 2, 1875.

7 Children of **David**, son of William 2d.

DAVID JR., left no children, lost seven.

PARMELA, married —— Graves.

SARAH, married —— Stone.

17 SAMUEL, born Dec. 1769, died Sept. 1835 ; married Clarissa Smith.

JOHN, no children.

REBECCA.

MARY.

7 Children of **Eliakim**, son of William 2d. Deerfield.

17 ELIAKIM JR., born 1767, (called Captain), married Tabitha Leonard. South Deerfield.

MARY, born 1769, (called Polly), never married. South Deerfield.

35 ESTHER, born 1772, died June 20, 1853, married Samuel Wells and Deacon Elihu Clary. Deerfield.

36 CHARLOTTE, born 1774, married Judah Wright.

18 SUSANNAH, born 1776, died Feb. 25, 1865 ; married Dr. Willard Arms, (page 11) son of Josiah. Brattleboro, Vt.

36 ABIGAIL, born 1780, died Jan. 12, 1854 ; married Elijah Sanderson. Charlemont, Mass.

FIFTH GENERATION.

8 Children of **Josiah**, son of Major John. Brattleboro, Vt.
WILLARD, died in infancy.
SUSANNAH, died aged 16 years.
18 JOHN, (Capt.) b. Aug. 11, 1776, d. July 23, 1825 ; m. Clarissa Steb-
    bins Nov. 29, 1797, who died Sept. 17, 1841. Brattleboro, Vt.
JOSIAH, died aged 12 years.
19 HANNAH, married Daniel Arms, son of Aaron. Brattleboro, Vt.
18 WILLARD, (Dr.) died aged 83, married Susannah Arms (page 10),
    daughter of Eliakim. West Brattleboro, Vt.
36 LUCINDA, married David Horton. Fabius, N. Y.
18 DANIEL (Dr.), born Aug. 31, 1786, died Sept. 8, 1840 ; married Eu-
    nice Gregory Sept. 16, 1809. Milford, Mich.
36 CYNTHIA, married Daniel Goodnow. Sherman, N. Y.
36 SYBIL, died 1873, married William Goodnow and Solomon Whitney.
    Kansas.
ELISHA, died aged 26, unmarried. Brattleboro, Vt.
18 WILLIAM, died 1876, married Polly Frost. Dummerston, Vt.
EDWIN, died aged 3 years. Brattleboro, Vt.
ANGELINA, married Rufus Hosley. Pennsylvania.

8 Children of **Aaron**, son of Daniel.
19 DANIEL, born Nov. 1776, married Hannah Arms, daughter of Josiah.
    Brattleboro, Vt.
19 CHRISTOPHER TYLER, born March, 1781, died July, 1854 ; married
    Avice Stebbins.
MARY, born Dec. 1784.
LUCY, born Nov. 1786, died Aug. 1840.
19 AARON, JR., born March, 1789, married Sophia Holland and Eliza
    Hapgood.
19 RALPH, born March, 1791, died Aug. 1851 ; married Caroline Bard-
    well. Deerfield.
SOPHIA, born October, 1794, died January, 1857.
36 MARTHA, born July, 1801, married Joshua Pratt. Deerfield.

8 Children of **Moses**, son of Ebenezer. Greenfield.
19 MOSES, JR., born 1785, died April, 1823. Greenfield.
IRA, born about 1783, d. aged 82 ; no children. Shelburn, Mass.
DOLLY.
CATHERINE.

8 Children of **Ebenezer, Jr.,** son of Ebenezer. Greenfield.

ELIZABETH, (called Betsey) born Dec. 8, 1785, died March 10, 1875 ; married Mr. Childs and Col. Long. Caledonia, N. Y.

19 CHESTER, born Sept. 13, 1787, died April 13, 1869 ; married Rebecca Goodman. Greenfield, Mass.

36 MARY, born Jan. 12, 1790, died Sept. 14, 1850 ; married Rev. William Goodell, D. D. 1815.

36 HARRIET, born Sept. 13, 1792, died Feb. 13, 1836 ; married Gen. Thos. D. Gilbert, 1814. Amherst, Mass.

36 EVOE, born June 21, 1794, died Nov. 23, 1853 ; married Eurotas Hastings, her cousin. Geneva, N. Y.

36 SOPHIA, born Sept. 8, 1802, m. Wm. A. Van Vranken, Geneva, N. Y.

EBENEZER WHITE, born March 29, 1805, died 1877 ; married Lydia Avery Nov. 12, 1835 ; had no children ; lawyer in Aurora, N. Y.

20 ROGER NEWTON, born Oct. 1806, died Nov. 16, 1852 ; married Lucretia Jane Taylor Dec. 27, 1838, who died in Philadelphia.

8 Children of **Jesse,** son of Ebenezer, all born in Duxbury, Vt.

20 IRA, born April 30, 1798, died April 23, 1862 ; married Parmelia Atherton, Feb. 5, 1821, who died April 25, 1862. Duxbury, Vt.

20 ORIN, born April 21, 1801 ; married Cynthia Hubbard, Sept. 1831, who died Dec. 19, 1843 ; married Elizabeth Stephens, March 15, 1846. Attica, Ind.

20 CHARLES C., M. D., born April 25, 1803, died April 18, 1854 ; married Lucia —— Waterbury, Vt.

LUCRETIA, born June 26, 1805, died June, 1836, at Waterbury, Vt. ; married O. W. Drew, M. D., who died 1876. Acton, Mass.

20 ALBERT, born Sept. 21, 1806 ; married Julia Ann Cushman, Dec. 9, 1832, and Mrs. Helen Kendall, January 4, 1862. Kendall, Mich.

EMILY, b. July 6, 1808, d. June 17, 1871, m. Alanson Chapin, St. Louis.

NORMAN, born Dec. 27, 1809, died March 13, 1816.

LAURA, born Dec. 24, 1811 ; m. Theodore Kendall. Janesville, Wis.

ESTHER, born Feb. 11, 1814 ; married Wm. Wells, of Greenfield, Mass. Manchester, Iowa.

ALONZO NORMAN, born June 16, 1816 ; died Nov. 19, 1862, in U. S. Army, 5th Michigan Volunteers.

AMBROSE, born March 9, 1818. No children. Chicago, Ill.

JESSE, JR., born July 31, 1820.

8 Children of **Daniel,** son of Consider.

CONSIDER, born November 17, 1794 ; died in infancy.

20 ISRAEL, born April 18, 1796, at Conway, Mass. ; died Oct. 20, 1838 ; married Sarah Axtell, May 8, 1819, who d. Feb. 1869. Sodus, N. Y.

36 MARIA H., born Sept. 25, 1798 ; married Henry D. Chapman and Hugh Montague. Unadilla, Mich.

MORRIS, b. Oct. 28, 1801, d. 1870 ; m. Almyra Pollock. No children.

21 FOSTER B., b. March 23, 1805 ; m. Mary A. Axtell, Fredonia, N. Y.

CHARLOTTE, born April 15, 1808 ; died April 15, 1808.
21 WILLIAM EDWIN, b. Oct. 9, 1815 ; m. Cynthia Brown. Pavilion, Mich.
21 LAWSON, born Nov. 4, 1817; married Harriet A. Paddock. Sodus, N.Y.
CHARLES A., born February 27, 1821 ; married Elizabeth Smith. No
children. Cold Spring, Minn.

8 Children of **Henry**, son of Consider. All born in Conway, Mass.
PHILENA, born Oct. 19, 1798, died June 10, 1838 ; married — Field,
October 15, 1818. Conway, Mass.
36 MARINDA, born August 31, 1800, died Oct. 8, 1872 ; married Augustus
Wells, June, 1926. Deerfield, Mass.
ELIZA, born February 9, 1802, died July 7, 1860 ; married Ichabod
Nelson, May 20, 1832. — — Mich.
LUCINDA, born May 18, 1804 ; married — Barker, August 16, 1837,
and Samuel Stebbins. Conway, Mass.
21 CONSIDER, born March 8, 1806 ; married Electa Boyden, June 4,
1839. Conway, Mass.
21 HENRY, JR., born Jan. 29, 1808 ; married Lucy Hamilton, June 16,
1839. Knoxville, Ill.
21 FRANKLIN, born Nov. 5, 1809; married Mary Williams, April 26,
1837. Conway, Mass.
21 CEPHAS, b. Oct. 5, 1811 ; m. Hannah Clark, June 17, 1839, who died
May 25, 1844 ; m. Louisa A. Taylor, Jan. 23, 1845. Knoxville, Ill.
FANNY, b. July 19, 1814; m. Geo. Stearns, Jan. 1, 1834. Conway, Mass.
21 OLIVER, born March 26, 1816 ; married Elizabeth Sprague, Sept. 12,
1840, and Nancy Ann Williams, Dec. 28, 1847. —— Tenn.
22 WILLIAM, born March 31, 1818 ; married Ann Eliza Smith, August
7, 1845. Knoxville, Ill.
CLARISSA, born May 9, 1820 ; married Edgar Metcalf, April 4, 1856.

9 Children of **John**, son of Consider, all born in Conway, Mass.
WEALTHY, born Aug. 1800 ; married Prof. Robert Coffin.
DOROTHY, born February, 1802.
22 ISRAEL, b. Feb. 28, 1804, d. Dec. 13, 1856; m. Julia Ann Parsons, May
28, 1825. Emigrated from Conway, Oct. 1826 to Brighton, Mich.
SOLOMON, born October, 1805. Never married.
JUDITH, born August, 1807. Married Edmund Burke.
JULIA ANN, born June, 1809. Married Rev. Mr. Ives.
JOHN, born September, 1811 ; died May 1836.
MARTHA, born March, 1813. Married Nelson Graves.
ELIJAH, born August, 1815. Never married.
CATHERINE, born October, 1816 ; died November, 1843.
MARY JANE, born February, 1818. Married Erastus Graves.
EDWARD, born February 1819 ; died February, 1829.
CORNELIA, born October, 1820. Married Augustus Graves.
CAROLINE, born August, 1823.

9 Children of **Christopher,** son of Consider.   Conway, Mass.

FRANCIS, born June 3, 1805 ; died July 27, 1805.

FRANCIS MARIA, born June 20, 1807 ; died July 5, 1807.

THOMAS ALLEN, born March 6, 1810.   Married Elizabeth Hawks.
No children.   Boston.

FREDERICK CLARY, born October 14, 1815.

FANNY, born July 24, 1817.

PAULINA, born August 28, 1819.

HARRIET, born October 13, 1823.

9 Children of **Oliver,** son of Consider.
Two daughters, now dead.

9 Children of **Abner,** son of Consider.

22 JOHN DWIGHT.   Died 1858, in Wisconsin.

CLARISSA.   Died in childhood.

CHARLES.   Died in childhood.

37 JANE MARIA, born February 17, 1820 ; married Rev. Samuel Adsit,
January 22, 1840.   Rochester, N. Y.

JAMES.   Drowned in 1832, aged 9 years.

37 ELIZABETH HAYDEN, born Sept. 3, 1828 ; married Rev. George
Plumer, Nov. 14, 1854, who died in the U. S. Army at New Orleans,
1864 ; married Andrew Harrington, 1872.   Boonville, N. Y.

37 ELIZA HAYS, born February 26, 1832 ; married Theodore Hale, Oct.
1862.   Canandaigua, N. Y.

9 Children of **Phineas,** son of William 3rd.

22 NOAH, born Feb. 1, 1783, died 1842 ; married Ruth Brand.

FANNY, born August 9, 1781 ; died July 17, 1785.

ACHSAH, born August 9 1785, died November, 1824 ; married David
Taylor ; no children.   Wyoming, Pa.

FANNY, born September, 1787 ; died February 21, 1788.

22 REV. SELAH ROOT, born February 21, 1789, died 1866 ; married
Eliza Ames.   Springfield, Vt.

ABIGAIL ROOT, born March 13, 1791 ; married Joseph Passamore.
Bradford Co., Pa.

23 PHINEAS, JR., born October 26, 1793 : m. Maria Bowles, Madison, Ia.

PHILIP ROOT, b. July 30, 1796, d. Mar. 1850, in N. Y. State ; no chld

IDDO, born Aug. 24, 1799 ; killed by Indians in Arkansas.

23 REV. WILLIAM, M. D., b. May 18, 1802 ; Class 1830, Amherst college;
studied theology at Andover ; married Mary Maxwell, April 6, 1835,
who died Dec. 19, 1835, Mary Ann Aiken, Jan. 8, 1839. Duquoin, IH.

MARY ANN, born May 18, 1802 ; died 1839.

ELIZABETH, born August 23, 1804 ; died July 9, 1806.

9 Children of **William 4th,** son of William 3rd.

23 WILLIAM 5TH, b. May, 1794, d. Feb. 1853; married Miranda Haven,
(p. 34) ; moved from Deerfield, 1814, to Sherbrooke, C. E.

DELIA, born 1795, died 1803. Goshen, Mass.

HIRAM, born 1797, died 1798, Windsor, Conn.

23 REV. HIRAM PHELPS, D. D., born at Windsor, Conn., June 1, 1799; married Lucy A. Wadhams, Sept. 12, 1824, who died July 3, 1837 ; married A. Jane Baker, Sept. 12, 1838. Graduated at Yale College in 1824 ; studied theology at the Divinity school of that college. Ordained pastor of the Congregational church at Hebron, Conn. June 30, 1830. Installed pastor of the church in Wolcottville, Conn., Feb. 6, 1833. Pastor of the First Church in Norwich, Conn., from August 3, 1836, to Feb. 10, 1873, when he resigned the active duties of his pastorate, but continued to reside among his people as Pastor Emeritus. In 1864, he received from the University of New York the degree of S. T. D., and in 1866 was chosen Fellow of Yale College. At the fiftieth anniversary of his graduation he reported to his class that "The evening of his uneventful life was passing pleasantly in a quiet home among a kind and affectionate people."

24 SENECA, born Nov. 16, 1806, at Ashfield, Mass.; married Nov. 6, 1833, Jane Wells, daughter of Samuel Wells and Esther Arms, (p. 34), daughter of Eliakim ; she died April 2, 1877. Moved from Deerfield in 1837 to Troy, N. Y. From 1848 to 1873 he was book-keeper for Mrs. Emma Willard's Seminary for young ladies—until the close of the institution.

JONATHAN, born 1809, died 1810. Newport, N. H.

9 Children of **Elijah, Jr.,** son of Elijah. South Deerfield.

EXPERIENCE, married Jonah Hawks.

AMELIA, married Artemus Williams.

MARTHA, married Austin Hawks.

PHILOMELA, married L. Loomis.

ESTHER, married — Allen.

ELECTA, married — Breese.

9 Children of **Eliphas,** son of Thomas. Deerfield.

HANNAH.   MELINDA.

24 ERASTUS, born July 23, 1785, died Dec. 17, 1830 ; married Mary Graham. Deerfield.

SOPHIA.

24 HARRY, born Aug. 30, 1787, died Sept. 13, 1855 ; married Fanny Hubbard May 4, 1820, who died Nov. 4, 1849. Deerfield.

25 DENNIS, born Aug. 4, 1790, died Jan. 18, 1854; married Betsey Richards and Mary Phelps. South Deerfield, Mass.

25 LEWIS, born Aug. 14, 1795, died Nov. 29, 1852 ; married Betsy Beales. Deerfield.

25 JOSIAH, b. March 15, 1800, d. March 26, 1842 ; m. Loana Graham, d. Sept. 25, 1828 ; m. Abigail Squares, d. March 28, 1869.

MARY.

9 Children of **Seth,** son of Thomas. Bernardston, Mass.

LUCRETIA, born 1784, died March 13, 1856; never married.

CLARISSA.

PATIENCE, baptized March 11, 1796.

LUCIUS, married Meletta Squires.

BETSEY. HENRY.

LEONARD, born 1796, died March 7, 1808.

ADMEY, married Oliver Harvey, March, 1817.

9 Children of **Thomas, Jr.,** son of Thomas. Deerfield.

MEHITABEL, born Oct. 22, 1786.

POLLY, born Feb. 9, 1789.

SENY, born Oct. 22, 1791.

DEXTER, born Oct. 29, 1797.

HARRIET, born Sept. 3, 1799, married Aaron Dickinson.

FIDELIA, born Nov. 26, 1801, married Squire Palmer April 23, 1830.

WEALTHY, born June 23, 1804, married Solomon Adkins.

JOHN BOYDEN, b. June 15, 1806, m. Hannah Childs April 17, 1836.

JOSIAH COOLRIDGE, born Sept. 23, 1808, married —— Bryant.

THOMAS ALVORD, born March 11, 1812.

JULIA ALMA, born Oct. 11, 1814, married Albert Clapp.

10 Children of **Rufus,** son of Thomas.

25 CAROLINE, d. Nov. 1834, m. Luman Arms, son Lemuel. Adams, N. Y.

LYMAN, died young.

SOPHRONIA, born June 1, 1799, m. Harry Sweetland. Portage, Mich.

ELECTA, died 1875, married Mr. Jones, Ypsilanti, Mich.

EMILY, died 1826, married James Plato. Rockford, Ill.

WILLIAM S., Wampsville, N. Y.

10 Children of **Lemuel,** son of Thomas.

25 RICHARD, born Jan. 1793, died 1865 ; m. Miss Thompson. Buffalo.

25 LUMAN, born Aug. 30, 1796, married Caroline Arms, daughter of Rufus. Adams, N. Y.

25 HIRAM, born Jan. 1799, died Feb. 1873. Adams, N. Y.

JOHN, never married. Adams, N. Y.

SARAH, married James Plato. Rockford, Ill.

LOUISE, never married.

——, married Mr. King. California.

10 Children of **Jonathan, Jr**, son of Jonathan. Montpelier, Vt.

25 STEPHEN. Boston, Mass.

25 AUSTIN, died Nov. 19, 1820; married Sally Davis Dec. 25, 1816, who died July 21, 1819. Montpelier, Vt.

37 SARAH, married Col. Jonathan P. Miller, of Greek fame.

10 Children of **Pliny,** son of Jonathan.

FREDERICK, born Sept. 30, 1811, died Oct. 11, 1811.

FREDERICK, born May 27, 1813, died Sept. 29, 1835.

JONATHAN, born March 18, 1815 ; died August 10, 1815.

37 MARTHA, born Sept. 28, 1817 ; married Henry Hitchcock, June 9, 1841. Galesburg, Ill.

JONATHAN, born July 19, 1819 ; died August 27, 1823.

37 THERESE THANKFUL, b. Mar. 17, 1821; m. George Herbert. Chicago.

25 JONATHAN DICKINSON, born Sept. 8, 1823 ; married Harriet Hitchcock. Monmouth, Ill.

WILLIAM, born Feb. 28, 1826 ; died May 24, 1835.

10 Children of **George,** son of Jonathan.

GEORGE, born 1828 ; died May 31, 1842. Glens Falls, N. Y.

10 Children of **Josiah Lyman,** son of Jonathan. Glens Falls, N.Y.

29 REV. JOSIAH LYMAN, b. Jan. 22, 1811; ordained Congregational clergyman, 1847 ; married Marcia K. Keith, Aug. 8, 1841, Woodstock, C.

ANNA HUNT, born Nov, 19, 1813 ; died Nov. 6, 1818.

ISABELLA, born May 26, 1817 ; died July 29, 1861.

LEWIS LYMAN, born Dec. 24, 1818 ; married Julia A. McDonald, Sept. 10, 1844. Glens Falls, N. Y.

ANNA HUNT, b. Feb. 19, 1821 ; m. Albert A. Cheney. Glens Falls.

FREDERICK AUGUSTUS, born May 19, 1823 ; died 1835.

26 GEORGE, born December 31, 1827, Muskegon, Mich.

10 Children of **Samuel,** son of David.

REV. CLIFFORD S., born 1796 ; died 1865. Orange Co., N. Y.

26 WALTER, born August, 1798 ; died November, 1872. Troy, N. Y.

26 SYLVESTER, born May, 1801. Unadilla, N. Y.

26 STILLMAN E., C. E., M. D., born November 1803, died July 10, 1877 ; married Rebecca English, 1832. Elizabeth, N. J.

26 SAMUEL, JR., born June, 1808 ; died 1870.

CLARISSA S., born April, 1813. Canaan, N. Y.

10 Children of **Eliakim, Jr.,** son of Eliakim. South Deerfield.

26 NOADIAH LEONARD, died 1841 ; married Hannah Gillings, who died in 1875. Albany, N. Y.

37 JERUSHA SMITH, married William Abel. Scotch Plains, N. Y.

37 HARRIET, born 1798, died 1846 ; m. Levi Williams. Albany, N. Y.

26 ORRAMEL, born Feb. 5, 1795, died August 3, 1876 ; married Olive Smith, September 14, 1822. Lansing, Mich.

38 ELIZA BRIDGMAN, b. 1804, at Ashfield, Mass.; m. Levi Cook. N. Y.

27 CHARLES, born 1806, died Nov. 14, 1871 ; married Harriet Morrell, Mary F. Thompson, November, 1858. Brooklyn, N. Y.

38 MARIA, born 1809 ; married Cyrus Carleton, 1829, who died in the West Indies; married Samuel Wells, 1851.

MIRANDA, born 1809 ; died 1821. Deerfield.

27 JAMES BOWDOIN, born Aug. 4, 1801 ; married Clarissa Smith, 1827. moved from Deerfield to Michigan in 1834. Dexter, Mich.

3

SIXTH GENERATION.

11 Children of **Capt. John,** son of Josiah. Brattleboro, Vt.

HENRY, born Oct. 13, 1798 ; died January 16, 1799.

28 JOSIAH, b. Dec. 24, 1799 ; m. Laura Shepardson. East Guilford, Vt.

28 JOHN, JR., born Oct. 7, 1801, died March 18, 1875 ; married Charlotte Hosley. Gill, Mass.

28 ALFRED, born June 7, 1804, died ——— ; married Gracia Greenleaf. East Guilford, Vt.

28 HINSDALE, born April 11, 1808, died June 12, 1866 ; married Theda Butterfield, who died March 9, 1870. Brattleboro, Vt.

28 WILLIAM, born July 25, 1811, d. 1866 ; m. Elizabeth Wadley. East Guilford, Vt.

11 Children of **Dr. Willard,** son of Josiah. Brattleboro, Vt.

38 CHARLOTTE, b. 1804, d. 1861 ; m. Oliver Matoon. Northfield, Mass.

28 WILLARD, JR., born 1806 ; married Gratia Liscom, 1837, and Diantha Cobleigh, 1864. Brattleboro, Vt.

EDWIN, born 1808 ; died 1826. Brattleboro, Vt.

38 SUSAN E., born 1816 ; m. Rev. Edward Wright, 1843, Rev. Jason Atwater, 1858. Principal Oak Hill Seminary. West Haven, Conn.

SARAH D., born 1818 ; died 1828. Northfield, Mass.

11 Children of **Dr. Daniel,** son of Josiah. Milford, Mich.

28 ANSLEY SHERWOOD, born Nov. 30, 1810, died June 2, 1874 ; married Catharine Laura Mead, December 21, 1835. Milford, Mich.

TWINS, died in infancy.

JANE GREGORY, born May 23, 1818 ; died June 3, 1828.

28 WILLIAM AVERY, born Aug. 31, 1821 ; m. Elsina Miranda Robinson. Aug. 24, 1844, who died Dec. 3, 1855, married Margaret Ann Wells, June 23, 1856. Milford, Mich.

29 WILLARD BURRITT, born Feb. 12, 1827; m. Lucretia Tuttle, May, 1853, who d. August, 1863 ; m. Eliza Ann Whitney, Feb. 10, 1864. Was twice a member of Michigan Senate. Chicago, Ill.

11 Children of **William,** son of Josiah. Dummerston, Vt.

38 SOPHIA, married Joseph Miller, 1844. Dummerston, Vt.

JERRY, born Dec. 27, 1819, d. Sept. 8, 1868 ; married Emiline Rider, May 26, 1845 ; no children. Clarkville, N. Y.

LESTINA, married John C. Millendy. Pleasanton, Kan.

38 MARY, married Alfred S. Brown. Guilford, Vt.

11 Children of **Daniel,** son of Aaron.
SUNNAH, born October 21, 1799.
38 CYNTHIA, born May 20, 1801 ; married Curtis Freeman.
AARON, born May 18, 1803.
38 LUCY, born March 18, 1808 ; married John Holden.
38 MARY, born Dec. 22, 1815 ; married Windsor Goddard.
29 RALPH, born April 19, 1818 ; married Mary Allis. So. Granby, P. Q.
38 SOPHIA, born July 11, 1823 ; married John Avery.
38 MARTHA, born January 28, 1827 ; married Luther Blunt.

11 Children of **Christopher Tyler,** son of Aaron.
ALBERT.
MELISSA, born May 24, 1807 ; married Stephen Allen.
JEANNETTE, born May 19, 1809 ; married A. Goodenough.
ALBERT, born April 9, 1811 ; died April 30, 1811.
ALBERT, born November 17, 1812 ; died March 20, 1813.
29 CHRISTOPHER TYLER, JR., born March 29, 1813 ; married Lucinda
Hayden, July, 1841. Columbus, O.
29 GEORGE ALBERT, b. Mar.7, 1815; m. Eunice Moody. Greenfield, Mass.
AVICE STEBBINS, born December 4, 1816.
29 RICHARD CATLIN, C. E., born October 29, 1818. Deerfield, Mass.
JULIA, born December 15, 1820 ; married Emerson Saunders.
MARIA, born July 31, 1823 ; died September 14, 1823.

11 Children of **Aaron, Jr.,** son of Aaron.
HUTCHINS H., born Oct. 15, 1827, died July 10, 1845 ; no children.
ELIZABETH, born 1830.
SOPHIA HOLLAND, born 1835.

11 Children of **Ralph,** son of Aaron. Deerfield.
29 OTIS B., born Nov. 15, 1816; married Sarah Wotkins, Aug. 16, 1842.
Bellows Falls, Vt.
29 JOHN, born May 29, 1819 ; married Mary B. Cragin, May 5, 1845.
CAROLINE S., born Oct. 10, 1820 ; m. Samuel H. Guild, June, 1857.
29 DANIEL, born Feb. 2, 1823 ; married Susan Gowdy, 1857.
ABBY FOSTER, born Sept. 17, 1825 ; m. F. M. Ball, April 2, 1857.
29 AARON, born August 23, 1829 ; married Mary J. Towns, Dec. 1855.
Bellows Falls, Vt.
EDWARD, born October 1, 1832 ; died March 15, 1843.
MARY ANN JACKSON, b. Sept. 6, 1836; m. F. M. Wilson, Feb. 24, 1856

11 Children of **Moses, Jr.,** son of Moses. Greenfield, Mass.
29 GEORGE W., b. Feb. 17, 1814 ; m. Julia Johnson, June 22, 1839, who
d. Nov. 1848 ; m. Abby T. Newton, Oct. 29, 1849. N.Vineland, N.J.
30 MOSES, JR., born March 26, 1820 ; police officer. San Francisco.

12 Children of **Chester,** son of Ebenezer, Jr. Greenfield, Mass.
30 ELIHU G., born May 10, 1821 ; married Susan B. J. Chandler, Jan.
20, 1848. Greenfield, Mass.

12 Children of **Roger Newton,** son of Ebenezer, Jr.

JOHN TAYLOR, born July 25, 1846. Washington, D. C.

38 MARY RAYMOND, b. Dec. 22, 1840; m. Otis Bigelow.   Washington.

ELIZABETH QUINTAN, born February 19, 1849.

ROGER NEWTON, JR., born April 26, 1853. New York.

12 Children of **Ira,** son of Jesse, all born in Duxbury, Vt.

30 CURTIS N., born Dec. 31, 1821 ; married Elizabeth L. Barber, Aug. 1847, and Sarah L. Hutchins, April, 1851. Waterbury, Vt.

30 PHILO, b. June 14, 1824; m. Ann E. Eddy, Oct. 3, 1849. Duxbury, Vt.

30 GEORGE C., born March 2, 1827 ; married Abby A. Mitchell, March 20, 1850. Waterbury, Vt.

MARY L., b. June 9, 1830; m. Isaac Wells, Aug. 4, 1853. Duxbury,Vt.

LUCRETIA D., born Sept. 1, 1835, died Aug. 18, 1856 ; married T. C. Lamson, September, 1853.

12 Children of **Orin,** son of Jesse. Attica, Ind.

39 LUCETTA, born July 1, 1832 ; married Thomas F. Payne, Oct. 28, 1852. Wabash, Ind.

30 SOLON H., b. Dec. 6, 1833; m. Diana Kell, Jan. 17, 1867. Benton, Ind.

AZRO A., born Dec. 5, 1835 ; no children. Rantout, Ill.

39 LAURA A., b. Aug. 25, 1837; m. John Dungan, Dec. 1, 1864. Benton Co., Ind.

IRA O., born December 12, 1843. Attica, Ind.

39 AMANDA, born Jan 29, 1847 ; m. Benjamin F. Bruck, Mar. 1, 1866.

39 CYNTHIA A., b. Oct. 13, 1848; m. Herman W. Timmons, Jan. 4, 1872.

CHARLES T., born Jan. 15, 1854 ; died November 28, 1857.

12 Children of **Dr. Charles C.,** son of Jesse. Waterbury, Vt.

CHARLES C. JR., M. D., born 1835 ; no children.

ELLA.

12 Children of **Albert,** son of Jesse. Kendall, Mich.

39 JULIA ANN, born February 25, 1834 ; married Martin Metcalf, June 7, 1857. Battle Creek, Mich.

LUCRETIA DREW, born November 29, 1836. Milwaukee, Wis.

MARY AUGUSTA, born November 25, 1838 ; died August 9, 1839.

39 MARGARET AUGUSTA, born January 25, 1844 ; married Jeremiah H. Anderson, March 22, 1865. Grand Rapids, Mich.

12 Children of **Israel,** son of Daniel. Sodus, N. Y.

39 JANE MARIA, born March 2, 1821 ; married Jos. B. Wilder, Jan. 5. 1842. Youngstown, O.

30 MYRON ISRAEL, born September 27, 1822 ; married Emeline C. Warner, November 29, 1848. Youngstown, O.

30 FREEMAN OSCAR, born April 14, 1824 ; married Emily S. Proceus, Sept. 18, 1849 ; m. Emily Wick, Nov. 21, 1865. Youngstown, O.

31 CHARLES DAYTON, born April 29, 1826 ; married Hannah M. Wick, May 27, 1852. Youngstown, O.

39 SOPHIA BIGELOW, born August 4, 1832 ; married Henry Manning, May 24, 1854. Youngstown, O.

HARRISON, born February 4, 1837 ; died Dec. 4, 1838. Sodus, N. Y.

12 Children of **Foster B.**, son of Daniel. Fredonia, N. Y.
SPENCER L., born November 23, 1836 ; died October 29, 1839.
BIGELOW M., born November 11, 1839 ; no children. Chicago, Ill.
MARY C., born November 11, 1841 ; m. F. W. Gage, Nov. 9, 1869.

13 Children of **William Edwin,** son of Daniel. Pavilion, Mich.
ARTHUR MASON, born March 31, 1852. Pavilion, Mich.

13 Children of **Lawson,** son of Daniel. Sodus, N. Y.
WILFORD P., born December 14, 1861. Sodus, N. Y.
CASTELLE J., born May 5, 1866. Sodus, N. Y.
CARRIE L., born January 29, 1869. Sodus, N. Y.

13 Children of **Consider,** son of Henry. Conway, Mass.
LUTHER BOYDEN, born March 17, 1840.
WILLIAM E., born September 25, 1843 ; died October 23, 1843.
ARTHUR C., born October 15, 1849.

13 Children of **Henry, Jr.,** son of Henry. Knoxville, Ill.
40 MATTIE H., born August 18, 1843 ; married Albert Mann, December 19, 1867. Knoxville, Ill.
31 HENRY W., born Oct, 1850 ; m. Eva Clark, Oct. 1870. Galesburg, Ill.

13 Children of **Franklin,** son of Henry. Conway, Mass.
31 WILLIAM ALDIS, born October 18, 1839 ; married Martha Cornell, June 6, 1870. Chicago.
31 GEORGE FRANKLIN, born August 12, 1842, died December 2, 1875 ; married May Filkins, July 7, 1870. Chicago.
CHARLES WILLIAMS, born April 23, 1838 ; died May 31, 1863.
GILBERT WHEELER, b. June 20, 1846 ; m. Lois Baker, April 24, 1872.
HORACE WILLIAMS, b. Oct. 28, 1853, m. Lottie Hayden, Nov. 9, 1875.

13 Children of **Cephas,** son of Henry. Knoxville, Ill.
31 CHARLES HENRY, born Dec. 25, 1840 ; married Aura B. Clark, Oct. 17, 1867. Dubuque, Ia.
JULIA HANNAH, born May 21, 1844 ; married George M. Barber, August 27, 1874. Chicago.

13 Children of **Oliver,** son of Henry. Tennessee.
31 JAMES HENRY, born Sept. 7, 1841 ; married Elizabeth Williams.
40 EMILY LOUISE E., born Feb. 7, 1843 ; married Wm. R. Berryhill.
SUSAN ANN, born August 11, 1848.
40 SARAH GATES, b. Jan. 1, 1850; m. Ransom P. Thompson, Feb. 9, 1873.
40 FANNY MELISSA, born Nov. 5, 1851 ; m. Waid Green, Sept. 6, 1873.

ISABELLA, born June 6, 1854.
WILLIAM FRANKLIN, born November 1, 1856.
JONATHAN, born January 9, 1859.
OLIVER, JR., born June 25th, 1860.
OSCAR, born June 25, 1860.

13 Children of **William**, son of Henry. Knoxville, Ill.
31 HENRY GATES, born May 15, 1846; married Mary F. Dunham, June 13, 1873. Albany, Kan.
ALBERT CEPHAS, born March 28, 1849. Knoxville, Ill.
CLARA AMELIA, born July 24, 1852. Knoxville, Ill.
BRAINARD ORTON, born December 15, 1855. Knoxville, Ill.

13 Children of **Israel**, son of John. Brighton, Mich.
HARRIET A., born April 4, 1826, married Rev. Sylvester Calkins, May 29, 1849. South Lyon, Mich.
31 JOHN, born Nov. 6, 1828, married Martha Jane Crane Dec. 21, 1851. Putnam, Mich.
40 NANCY ELVIRA, born June 20, 1830, married Seth Bidwell Dec. 19, 1850. Brighton, Mich.
40 ELEANOR PILCHER, born May 18, 1832, married Elisha Avery Calkins April 24, 1855. South Lyon, Mich.
31 HENRY COLCHAZER, born April 8, 1834, married Elsina Glines Nov. 15, 1857, who died March 10, 1875 ; married S. Eugenia Goodspeed Sept. 27, 1876. Decatur, Mich.
32 EDWIN ISRAEL, born Feb. 7, 1840, married Alice May Grady July 4, 1868. South Lyon, Mich.
JULIA ANN, born Aug. 20, 1842, died May 22, 1873 ; married Hugh Taylor Smith Aug. 26, 1869. New Hudson, Mich.
40 CATHERINE ROSELLA, born July 2. 1846, married Joshua Harker Nov. 9, 1869. South Lyon, Mich.

14 Children of **John Dwight**, son of Abner.
One child.

14 Children of **Noah**, son of Phineas.
32 NELSON J., born 1805, married Hannah Otteburn, d. 1831, Eliza Beals, d. 1839, and Sarah Hancox. Albany, N. Y.
HIRAM H., born 1807, died 1847 ; married Eliza Williams.
WAIT, born 1808, married Julia Sheldon.
SELAH R., born 1810, married Margaret Butler.
FANNY L. R., born 1812, died 1842 ; married Foster B. Wilson.
WILLIAM H. A., born 1815, married Louisa ———

14 Children of **Rev. Selah Root**, son of Phineas. Springfield, Vt.
WILLIAM JAMES, born Feb. 7, 1826.
MARIA PHŒBE, born Aug. 7, 1827. Springfield, Mass.
40 ELIZA, b. Dec. 28, 1828, m. John F. Moseley. Springfield, Mass.
GEORGE, born Dec. 12, 1829. Machinist, not married. New York.

FANNY, b. Jan. 14, 1832, m. Daniel Goddard. Westminster, Vt.

EMILY, born Nov. 15, 1833, died Sept. 1834. Livingstonville, N. Y.

EMILY MAXWELL, born May 12, 1835. Springfield, Mass.

NATHAN PEABODY, born July 2, 1837. Springfield, Vt.

EBENEZER BURGESS, born March 13, 1839, died in U. S. army.

HENRY MARTIN, born Aug. 17, 1840, m. Sarah —— Limeron, N. M.

ELLEN AMELIA, born April 7, 1842. Teacher. Sandwich Islands.

14 Children of **Phineas, Jr.**, son of Phineas. Madison, Iowa.

WILLIAM, ELIZABETH, EDWARD PAYSON, LYDIA, GEORGE, WILLIS
TON, MINERVA.

14 Children of **Rev. William, M. D.**, son of Phineas. Duquoin, Ill.

WILLIAM GOODWIN, b. April 17, 1842, d. in U. S. army Aug. 4, 1863.

40 MARY ELIZABETH, b. Dec. 17, 1845, m. Jas. G. Milligan, Aug. 19,'63.

MARIA SARAH, born Jan. 25, 1847, died Sept. 18, 1867.

40 EMILY PIERCE, b. June 11, 1849, m. Luman P. Parker Aug. 3, 1870.

14 Children of **William 5th**, son of William 4th. Sherbrooke, C. E.

40 ADELINE, born 1821 ; married Samuel Tuck. Sherbrooke, C. E.

DELIA, born 1823.

MIRANDA, born 1827 ; married Thomas Goldsmith. Troy, N. Y.

40 ADELIA, born 1829 ; married John McNickle. Sherbrooke, C. E.

40 CALISTA, born 1831 ; married Lemuel Farwell. Sherbrooke, C. E.

32 WILLIAM 6TH, born 1834 ; married Mary Street. Sierra Valley, Cal.

15 Children of **Rev. Hiram P., D. D** , son of William 4th. Norwich, Conn.

CATHERINE LEWIS, born 1825, died 1826.

CATHERINE LEWIS, born 1827, died 1828.

40 CATHERINE BRUYN, born August 29, 1828 ; m. Luther P. Fisher, October 11, 1859. Oakland, Cal.

32 REV. WILLIAM FREDERIC, born February 26, 1831. Graduated at Yale College, 1853 ; studied theology at Andover, Mass. Married, January 3, 1860, Emily Meekins, of Greenfield, Mass. Ordained at Boston as missionary of the American Board to Turkey. On the death of his wife he returned to this country. Married, March 3, 1863, Sarah Phelps, of Wilbraham, Mass. After brief pastorates at Greenwich and Newton, Conn., Nicholson, Pa., and Bemerville, N. J., he was installed Pastor of the Congregational Church in Sunderland, Mass., December 1, 1875.

32 GEORGE HENRY, C. E., born April 15, 1833 ; married Henrietta Mackay, December 26, 1853.

32 FRANK HIRAM, born June 1, 1835 ; married Grace Turner, April 11, 1865. Paymaster U. S. Navy.

40 LUCY ANN, born May 17, 1837, died June 30, 1865 ; married Edwin A. Berry, February 16, 1859. Terre Haute, Ind.

41 SARAH JANE, born Aug. 14, 1839, married Rev. Wm. B. Clarke, April 18, 1866. New Haven, Conn.

32 CHARLES JESSUP, born June 9, 1841 ; graduated at Yale College, 1863 ; served in the war of the rebellion as Captain in 20th Conn. Volunteers. Practiced law in Lewiston, Pa., but afterward changed his profession to journalism. Married Alice Avery, October 17, 1873. In 1876, was appointed on the staff of Gov. Hartranft, of Pennsylvania, with rank of Colonel. Lancaster, Pa.

32 THEODORE WINTHROP, born November 8, 1844 ; married Rose Marselis, October 13, 1869. Philadelphia.

15 Children of **Seneca**, son of William 4th. Troy, N. Y.

41 JENNIE ELIZABETH, born August 28, 1834, at Deerfield, died at Troy, March 26, 1862 ; married Rev. Wm. H. Taylor, September 8, 1858.

32 GEORGE WELLS, born May 17, 1837, at Deerfield ; married Jennie Van De Mark ; married Addie Fields, November 16, 1876. Philadelphia, Pa,

CHARLES HENRY, born Jan. 22, 1839, at Troy, married Sarah A. Hill, April 20, 1871. New York.

41 MATTIE HARRIET, born Aug. 12, 1842, at Troy ; died Dec. 6, 1873 ; married Charles K. Wallace. Brooklyn, N. Y.

32 EDWARD WRIGHT, born Dec. 4, 1845, at Troy ; graduated at the Rensselaer Polytechnic Institute in 1869, with the degree of Civil Engineer ; married Ella S. Wright, Jan. 11, 1871. Troy, N. Y.

15 Children of **Erastus**, son of Eliphas. Deerfield.

LAURAETT, born Nov. 27, 1814, died Sept. 16, 1832.

GEORGE WRIGHT, born May 24, 1816, died Sept. 1832.

ANGELINE, born Feb. 10, 1818, died Aug. 26, 1865.

SYLVIA, born March 25, 1820, married Samuel Hastings, May 7, 1840. Deerfield.

HORACE CORNWELL, b. May 8, 1822, married three times. Kansas.

ELIZA, born May 25, 1824, married Franklin Woodruff. Deerfield.

MARY AUGUSTA, born May 27, 1826, married Monroe Eldridge and John B. Yorbert, April 1871. Humboldt, Kansas.

DAVID BRAINARD, b. March 28, 1829, m. Julia C. Vail May 20, 1874. Deerfield.

15 Children of **Harry**, son of Eliphas. Deerfield.

32 ALBERT AUSTIN, born July 19, 1821, married Sabrina Packard, May 13, 1847. Deerfield.

LYMAN SPENCER, born Feb. 25, 1823, died —, married Diadamia Allen, Feb. 6, 1855.

33 WILLIAM, born Oct. 5, 1825, married Sultana Packard May 3, 1849. Deerfield.

DELIA, born 1830, married Chas. Brickman. Northampton, Mass.

AMELIA, born 1830, married Chas. Rogers. Leverett.

15 Children of **Dennis**, son of Eliphas. Deerfield.

33 WILLIAM SHEPARD, born March 22, 1819. Springfield, Mass.

33 JAMES C., born September 13, 1826. Northampton, Mass.

41 ELIZABETH RICHARDS, born August 1817; married Lewis H. Fellows, May 27, 1840. Deerfield.

33 CHARLES, born January 6, 1831, manufacturer. South Deerfield.

15 Children of **Lewis**, son of Eliphas. Deerfield.
HENRY, born December 17, 1830. Deerfield.
SARAH, born September, 1843. Deerfield.

15 Children of **Josiah**, son of Eliphas.
DIANTHA, b. July 13, 1823; d. April 16, 1845, m. Geo. Remington.
LOANA, born August 26, 1828; married ——

33 O. S., born Aug. 13, 1830; married Julia A. Wrisley, Nov. 25, 1852, d. August 3, 1860; m. Lecta A. Lovejoy, April 7, 1863. Deerfield.

16 Children of **Richard**, son of Lemuel. Buffalo, N. Y.
A DAUGHTER, died 1874; married A. A. Selover.
A DAUGHTER; married James Selover. New York.
RICHARD, JR. Sacramento, Cal.
WILLIAM, died 1873. Hong Kong, China.
JENNIE. JESSIE.

16 Children of **Luman**, son of Lemuel. Adams, N. Y.
LOUISA, born 1825, m. Albert Yenders. St. Joseph Co., Mich.
JULIA, b. 1827, married Merrick Needham.

33 WILLIAM D., born Feb. 14, 1829, married Lavinda Horton 1855, who died Aug. 1872. Adams, N. Y.

33 HENRY, born April 14, 1830, married Sarah Beardsley, 1851. Mich.
HARRISON, born August, 1840, married Lucy Wooley, Feb. 6, 1862; no children. Toledo, O.

33 FOSTER M., born 1843, married Fanny Barrows, 1867. Adams, N. Y.
GERTRUDE, born 1847, married Charles Heath. Adams, N. Y.

16 Children of **Hiram**, son of Lemuel. Adams, N. Y.
FOSTER, born 1826, died 1853.
JOHN, born 1827. Adams, N. Y.
EMELINE, born 1836, died April 1860; married Sanford Hunt 1856.

16 Children of **Stephen**, son of Jonathan, Jr. Boston.
SARAH, married Mr. Dwight. Weathersfield, Conn.

16 Children of **Austin**, son of Jonathan, Jr. Montpelier, Vt.

33 AUSTIN D., born Dec. 26, 1817, married Fanny Dodge, Jan. 14, 1841. Montpelier, Vt.

17 Children of **Jonathan Dickinson**, son of Pliny. Monmouth, Ill.
MARY THERESE, born July 31, 1854.
HARRIET NEWELL, born Dec. 21, 1856.
WILLIAM HENRY, born Sept. 22, 1858.
MARTHA HITCHCOCK, born Nov. 27, 1863.

4

17 Children of **Rev. Josiah Lyman,** son of Josiah L. Woodstock, C.
    CLARA ADELIA, born November 5, 1845.
41 ABBY LOUISA, born March 21, 1847 ; married Edwin B. Hosmer,
    September 11, 1864. Woodstock, Conn.
    ELLA MORTIMER, born December 25, 1849.
    ANNETTA FRANCES, born March 15, 1852.
    HENRY LYMAN, born May 31, 1854.
    WILLARD OTIS, born February 27, 1857.
    AZRA HERBERT, born January 22, 1860.
    MARCIA ALICE, born January 18, 1865.

17 Children of **George,** son of Josiah Lyman. Muskegon, Mich.
    LYMAN, born Nov. 3, 1853, at Glens Falls, N. Y.
    JOHN FASSETT, b. Oct. 1, 1856, d. Aug. 6, 1857. Grand Rapids, Mich.
    HELEN HUNT, born June 18, 1859, at Chicago.
    ANNA CHENEY, born May 7, 1863. Muskegon, Mich.
    FREDERICK FASSETT, born November 14, 1864. Muskegon, Mich.

17 Children of **Walter,** son of Samuel. Troy, N. Y.
41 ANTOINETTE, b. 1828, d. Dec. 1872 ; m. Joseph DeGolyer. Troy, N.Y.
    JENNIE, born 1830. Troy, N. Y.

17 Children of **Sylvester,** son of Samuel. Unadilla, N. Y.
    MOSES, died 1850.
    ELIZABETH,'married George King.
34 GILBERT, married Augustus Sluter. Virginia.
41 HENRIETTA, married Henry Foster.
    SYLVESTER, JR., married Agnes Burger.

17 Children of **Dr. Stillman E.,** son of Samuel. Elizabeth, N. J.
41 MARY ELIZABETH, born October, 1833 ; married Rev. W. T. Morri-
    son, missionary to China, who died 1869.
    SARAH JANE, born December, 1835.
    HENRY MARTIN, born September, 1838 ; died August, 1850.
41 AUGUSTA LOUISA, born August, 1845 ; m. Rev. Aaron Zabriskie.
    CLARA WARD, born August, 1847.

17 Children of **Samuel, Jr.,** son of Samuel.
34 CLIFFORD S., born January 1, 1834 ; married Fidelia Williams, Jan.
    10, 1865, who died May 25, 1872. Lawyer. Unadilla, N. Y.
    EDWARD P. Rockdale, N. Y.
    SARAH.   AMELIA.
    TAYLOR L. Lawyer, Unadilla, N. Y.

17 Children of **Noadiah Leonard,** son of Eliakim, Jr. Albany, N.Y.
41 MARIA, born 1825 ; married Jacob E. Parsons. Yonkers, N. Y.
41 HENRIETTA, born 1833, died October, 1872 ; married G. Dudley Van
    Vliet. Albany, N. Y.   ·
34 NELSON L., born 1839 ; married Amo Rett Goodale. New York.

17 Children of **Orramel,** son of Eliakim, Jr. Lansing, Mich.

EDWARD CHESTER, born Aug. 14, 1825. Lawyer ; went south.

HENRY BRIDGEMAN, born 1826. Died in infancy.

34 HENRY BRIDGEMAN, born Feb. 6, 1827 ; married Harriet D. Snyder. Oakland, Cal.

34 CHARLES WILLIAM, born December 20, 1828 ; married Susan Elvina Parker, June 26, 1864. Oakland, Cal.

34 GEORGE WELLS, born July 11, 1830; married Sarah Elizabeth Dallam, June 4, 1857. Oakland, Cal.

The last three spell their name ARMES.

17 Children of **Charles,** son of Eliakim, Jr. Brooklyn, N. Y.

EMILY MORRELL, born 1837 ; married F. L. Page. Oakland, Cal.

CHARLES ERNEST, born 1839 ; died 1864.

JAMES C., born 1841 ; died 1860.

FRANK ELDEN, born February 3, 1860. Brooklyn, N. Y.

CHARLES ERNEST, born March 11, 1865. Brooklyn, N. Y.

NELLIE HOWARD, born March 6, 1871. Brooklyn, N. Y.

17 Children of **James Bowdoin,** son of Eliakim, Jr. Dexter, Mich.

34 GEORGE CARLTON, born November 23, 1830, died June 4, 1876 ; married Dorlissa E. Dibble. Dexter, Mich.

34 CHARLES B., born Oct. 19, 1832 ; m. Amanda Williams. —— Ill.

34 JAMES BRIDGEMAN, born Dec. 11, 1838 ; married Cora E. Crorron. Dexter, Mich.

BENJAMIN FRANKLIN, born March 8, 1841, died June 2, 1864 ; killed in battle of Cold Harbor, Va.

SEVENTH GENERATION.

18 Children of **Josiah,** son of Capt. John. East Guilford, Vt.
ELLEN, married Alonzo Wetherland. Guilford, Vt.

18 Children of **John, Jr.,** son of Capt. John. Gill, Mass.
OSCAR, died at sea, aged 23 years.
JOHN, JR., born 1833 ; died July 15, 1855.
JOSEPH, married Abbie Harris. Gill, Mass.
BENJAMIN, unmarried.
CLARA, unmarried.
MARY, born 1835 ; died March 17, 1857.

18 Children of **Alfred,** son of Capt. John. East Guilford, Vt.
ALFRED, JR., died in U. S. Army.

18 Children of **Hinsdale,** son of Capt. John. Brattleboro, Vt.

34 ROBERT BRUCE, born September 21, 1834; married Fanny Lucretia
Thayer, Dec. 25, 1856. Capt. Co. B. 16th Regt. Vermont Vols. ;
now deputy Collector of Customs. Burlington, Vt.

34 EDWIN HERBERT, born Sept. 8, 1838 ; married Felicia Larissa Wil-
cox, June 2, 1864, who died May 9, 1868 ; married Myra Goodeve,
Nov. 3, 1870, who died April 27, 1876. Drummer, 4th Regt. Vermont Vols. Guelph, Ont.

18 Children of **William,** son of Capt John. East Guilford, Vt.
SARAH.

18 Children of **Willard, Jr.,** son of Dr. Willard. Brattleboro, Vt.
JANE ELIZA, b. 1839, d. 1864; m. Harrison Niles, 1863. Brattleboro.
GEORGE WILLARD, born 1843 ; died 1840. Brattleboro, Vt.
TWIN SON, born 1843; died 1843. Brattleboro, Vt.
GRATIA, died 1864. Brattleboro, Vt.

18 Children of **Ansley Sherwood,** son of Dr. Daniel. Milford, Mich.
ANSLEY MARSHALL, born February 3, 1837 ; died Sept. 10, 1837.
JANE GREGORY, born February 3, 1839 ; died June 14, 1840.
JANE MEAD, born January 31, 1842 ; died October 28, 1843.
ANSLEY WILLIAM, born January 1, 1844 ; married Mary Elizabeth
Scriver, June 9, 1866 Wixom, Mich.
WILLARD ANSLEY, born October 8, 1848. Novi, Mich.

18 Children of **William Avery,** son of Dr. Daniel. Milford, Mich.
42 AMELIA GREGORY, born January 17, 1848 ; married Clark Crawford,
October 16, 1867. Pontiac, Mich.
ANSLEY ALBERT, born Aug. 26, 1850; married Mary Bennett, Oct.
19, 1871. Milford, Mich.

LILLIAN JOSEPHINE, born December 29, 1852 ; married Alfred P.
Lyon, February 25, 1875. Bay City, Mich.
WILLIAM ROBINSON, b. Sept. 28, 1855; d. Jan, 22, 1857. Milford, Mich.
EUNICE SOPHIA, b. June 28, 1858 ; died May 13, 1859. Milford, Mich.
CLARA WELLS, born June 8, 1861. Milford, Mich.
SANFORD AVERY, born February 12, 1867. Milford, Mich.

18 Children of **Hon. Willard Burritt,** son of Dr. Daniel. Chicago.
WILLIE BURRITT, born June 6, 1858, died July 5, 1875.
DANIEL, born Sept. 14, 1860.
NETTIE, born Nov. 8, 1864.
GEORGE, born Dec. 29, 1865.

19 Children of **Ralph,** son of Daniel.
JANE, born Aug. 15, 1847, married Edwin Holden. So. Granby, P. Q.
JOHN HALL, born January 22, 1850. South Granby, P. Q.
RALPH, JR., born March 23, 1853. South Granby, P. Q.
42 TISGAH, b. March 9, 1856 ; m. Almon Higgins. South Granby, P. Q.

19 Children of **Christopher Tyler, Jr.,** son of Christopher T.
CHRISTOPHER TYLER, 3D.
ISABELLA.
ANNA PRAGUE.
WALTER FRENCH.
RICHARD C.,

19 Children of **George Albert,** son of Christopher Tyler.
42 ELLEN LOUISA, born Nov., 1847 ; married John Shelder, Oct., 1871.
Greenfield, Mass.
JENNIE MARIA, born June, 1852. Greenfield, Mass.
GEORGE LOBDELL, born April, 1854. Greenfield, Mass.

19 Children of **Richard Catlin,** son of Christopher Tyler. Deerfield.
WINTHROP TYLER, born September 30, 1861.

19 Children of **Otis B.,** son of Ralph. Bellows Falls, Vt.
EDWARD, born May 14, 1843 ; married M. J. Holt, May 14, 1872.
LIZZIE, born July 25, 1852.

19 Children of **John,** son of Ralph.
GERTRUDE G., born May 5, 1849.

19 Children of **Daniel,** son of Ralph.
HENRY FULLERTON, born June 17, 1860.

19 Children of **Aaron,** son of Ralph.
LILLA J., born October 29, 1856.

19 Children of **George W.,** son of Moses, Jr. North Vineland, N. J.
ANNA, born April 7, 1840; died November, 1848.
EVA L., born September 3, 1853.
GEORGE W., JR., born June 19, 1855.

19 Children of **Moses 3d**, son of Moses Jr. San Francisco, Cal.

MOSES C. born February 25, 1851, at Racine, Wis.

EDGAR C., born January 8, 1856, at Petaluma, Cal.

WILLIAM H., born March 23, 1860, at Petaluma, Cal.

GEORGE W., born April 3, 1872, at San Francisco.

NETTIE, born January 17, 1876, at San Francisco.

TWO SONS and ONE DAUGHTER, died young.

19 Children of **Elihu G.**, son of Chester, all born in Greenfield, Mass.

HELEN B., born March 27, 1849; died July 27, 1871.

SARAH Z., born April 4, 1851; died July 6, 1873.

CHESTER, born April 3, 1857; died February 6, 1859.

MARY E., born July 16, 1859.

MARTHA G., born October 22, 1863.

20 Children of **Curtis N.**, son of Ira. Waterbury, Vt.

EDWIN W., born September 20, 1852; died April 28, 1858.

LILLIE M., born October 20, 1859.

20 Children of **Philo**, son of Ira. Duxbury, Vt.

ALICE L., born March 2, 1857; died February 10, 1862.

JESSE, born February 14, 1859.

ARTHUR, born March 16, 1863; died December 18, 1863.

MINNIE, born December 5, 1865.

20 Children of **George C.**, son of Ira. Waterbury, Vt.

IZZIE, born Nov. 9, 1851; married Geo. H. Mitchell, Feb. 19, 1873.

GEORGE H., born March 28, 1855.

IRA, born February 6, 1864; died March 16, 1875.

MILLIE, born April 16, 1867.

20 Children of **Solon H.**, son of Orin. Benton, Ill.

MARY G., born July 5, 1869.

ORIN S., born October 16, 1874.

20 Children of **Myron Israel**, son of Israel. Youngstown, O.

42 MARY, born October 18, 1849; married Henry Wick, Nov. 4, 1869. Youngstown, O.

MYRON ISRAEL, JR., born January 30, 1854.

WARNER, born Nov. 30, 1851; married Fannie Williamson Wick, February 17, 1875. Youngstown, O.

EMELINE ELIZA, born April 6, 1857.

JANE MARIA, born October 16, 1859.

HARRIET EXPERIENCE, born November 3, 1861.

20 Children of **Freeman Oscar**, son of Israel. Youngstown, O.

CARRIE LOUISE, born May 29, 1851.

FREEMAN PROCEUS, born March 3, 1856; died January 31, 1861. Youngstown, O.

21 Children of **Charles Dayton**, son of Israel, all born at Youngstown, O.

SARAH ADELIA, born January 30, 1853.
ANNA MARIA, born Sept. 2, 1855.
CATHERINE, born February 1, 1858.
CAROLINE WICK, born April 4, 1860.
LAURA BELLE, born Nov. 5, 1862.
OLIVE FREEMAN, born January 15, 1865.

21 Children of **Henry W.**, son of Henry, Jr. Galesburg, Ill.
CLAYTON.

21 Children of **William Aldis**, son of Franklin. Chicago.
HARRY CORNELL, born Aug. 2, 1873.

21 Children of **George Franklin**, son of Franklin. Chicago.
FRANKLIN, born March 11, 1872.

21 Children of **Charles Henry**, son of Cephas. Dubuque, Iowa.
HERBERT CLARK. CLARA LOUISA.

21 Children of **James Henry**, son of Oliver.
MAMANDA JANE, born March 6, 1864.
JAMES IRWIN, born April 5, 1866.
JOHN OLIVER, born 1868.
ROBERT LEE, born 1870.
NANCY EMILY, born 1872, died 1874.
LOUISA ELIZABETH, born 1874.

22 Children of **Henry Gates**, son of William. Albany, Kan.
CLARA AMELIA, born April 20, 1873.
WILLIAM HENRY, born Feb. 1, 1875.

22 Children of **John**, son of Israel. Putnam, Mich.
HARRIET LOUISA, born June 13, 1853 ; married H. T. Smith Sept. 10, 1874. Green Oaks, Mich.
MARY ALICE, born Aug. 31, 1854 ; married G. A. Liginan April, 1875. Brighton, Mich.
PHILINDA GASTON, born April 18, 1857, died May 16, 1860.
SYLVESTER CALKINS, born Nov. 25, 1858, died May 17, 1860.
CHESTER ELMER, born Aug. 6, 1861.
BERTHA ESTELLE, born Sept. 14, 1864.
CLARIA OLEATTA, born Sept. 18, 1866.
ELSIA LOIS, born April 26, 1870, died May 22, 1870.
EFFIA A., born July 17, 1871, died Sept. 8, 1871.
JOHN RAY, born Aug. 5, 1874.

22 Children of **Henry Colchazer**, son of Israel. Decatur, Mich.
FRANK A., born Jan. 22, 1859.

22 Children of **Edwin Israel,** son of Israel.   South Lyon, Mich.
ANNA VIOLA, born June 8, 1872.
LORENA LUELLA, born April 16, 1877.

22 Children of **Nelson J.,** son of Noah.   Albany, N. Y.
A DAUGHTER.

23 Children of **William 6th,** son of William 5th.   Sierra Valley, Cal.
WILLIAM ISAAC, born Jan. 1876, died Jan. 1876.

23 Children of **Rev. William Frederick,** son of Rev. Hiram P.,
D. D. Sunderland, Mass.
EMILY MEEKINS, born March 20, 1861.
CATHERINE PHELPS, born Sept. 15, 1865.
SARAH LUCY, born March 23, 1868.
WILLIAM WELLS, born Feb. 27, 1871, died March 10, 1875.
GEORGE ALBERT, born Feb. 3, 1874, died Oct. 23, 1875.

23 Children of **George Henry,** son of Rev. Hiram P., D. D.
HIRAM PHELPS, born Oct. 11, 1854.
SOPHIA NORRIS, born Sept. 24, 1856.
LOULIE WYETH, born Dec. 23, 1860.
FREDERICK WILLIAM, born June 3, 1862.
CHARLES, born Nov. 24, 1866.

23 Children of **Frank Hiram,** son of Rev. Hiram P., D. D. New
Bedford, Mass.
FRANK, born 1866.
ALICE WEAVER, born 1876.

24 Children of **Charles Jessup,** son of Rev. Hiram P., D. D. Lancaster, Pa.
LILY, born May 29, 1875.
AUDUBON, born 1876.

24 Children of **Theodore Winthrop,** son of Rev. Hiram P., D. D.
HELEN BAKER, born July 5, 1870.
LUCY, born Sept. 9, 1871.
THEODORE JESSUP, born March 9, 1873.

24 Children of **George Wells,** son of Seneca. Philadelphia.
CHARLES EDWARD, born June 22, 1860. Naval cadet—at sea.
JESSIE, born Dec. 1862, died July, 1863, at Albany, N. Y.

24 Children of **Edward Wright,** son of Seneca. Troy, N. Y.
LUCIUS WRIGHT, born December 8, 1873. Troy, N. Y.

24 Children of **Albert Austin,** son of Harry. Deerfield, Mass.
ALLISON, born September 7, 1847.
ALVAH C., born August 1850.
HUDSON, born January 9, 1852.
EVA, born January 21, 1854.
ALFORD, born July 24, 1856.

MINNIE, born May 27, 1858.
MONTREALL, born October 10, 1860.
GEORGE, born January 25, 1862.
LIZZIE, born April 18, 1865.
EUGENE, born April 22, 1867.

24 Children of **William,** son of Harry. Deerfield.
FANNY, born April 29, 1854.
WILLIAM, born February 6, 1860.
FRANK, born November 9, 1861.

25 Children of **O. S.,** son of Josiah. South Deerfield.
CARRIE LEETTA, born November 7, 1870.

25 Children of **William Shepard,** son of Dennis. Springfield, Mass.
ACHSAH MARIA, born December 20, 1848 ; married Alonzo M. Rice,
November 23, 1869. Deerfield.
MARY P., born July 1, 1854 ; died August 13, 1854.
MARY S., born October 7, 1855.
LILLIAN DENNIS, born March 11, 1861.
MARTHA WASHINGTON, born February 22, 1863.
NELLIE SHEPARD, born May 2, 1865.
WILLIAM SUMNER, born February 10, 1867.

25 Children of **James C.,** son of Dennis. Northampton, Mass.
ANNIE C., born November 26, 1860 ; died June 2, 1874.
JAMES DENNIS, born October 15, 1863.
EDITH LUCY, born February 16, 1868.
MARY WELLS, born August 26, 1869.
GRACE AGNES, born May 3, 1876.

25 Children of **Charles,** son of Dennis. South Deerfield.
JULIA MARIA, born June 28, 1853 ; m. Wm. W. Foster, June 5, 1872.
HATTIE ELIZABETH, born July 17, 1860.
MINNIE LINCOLN, born May 23, 1865.
EDWARD BARTLETT, born October 7, 1867.

25 Children of **William D.,** son of Luman. Adams, N. Y.
MINNIE I.., born May 23, 1859.
CARRIE L., born May 28, 1862.

25 Children of **Henry,** son of Luman. Michigan.
WILLIAM, born 1852.   TWO SONS.

25 Children of **Foster M.,** son of Luman. Adams, N. Y.
GEORGE, born 1868.

25 Children of **Austin D.,** son of Austin. Montpelier, Vt.
SARAH R., born February 3, 1842, died November 30, 1864; married
N. P. Dodge, May 29, 1862. San Francisco, Cal.
STEPHEN W., born September 21, 1844.
FANNY, born July 31, 1855.

5 `

26 Children of **Gilbert**, son of Sylvester. Virginia.
ADA.

26 Children of **Clifford S.**, son of Samuel, Jr. Unadilla, N. Y.
WILLIAW W., born November 2, 1865 ; died June 24, 1871.
SAMUEL, born May 1, 1872 ; died May 3, 1872.

26 Children of **Nelson L.**, son of Noadiah Leonard. New York.
GERTRUDE HAMILTON, born January 27, 1866.
CARRIE HOUGH, born February 9, 1871.

27 Children of **Henry Bridgeman**, son of Orramel. Oakland, Cal
MARY AMANDA, born January 26, 1856.
HATTIE GEORGIA, born December 15, 1858.
CHARLES WILLIAM, born February 5, 1860.

27 Children of **Charles William**, son of Orramel. Oakland, Cal.
GEORGE HENRY, born June 28, 1866.
SUSIE ELLA, born Nov. 8, 1867 ; died Aug. 7, 1868, at San Francisco.
CHARLES WILLIAM, JR., born June 2, 1869.

27 Children of **George Wells**, son of Orramel.
GEORGE WILLIAM DALLAM, born August 3, 1860.
HELEN FRANCES, b. April 18, 1862 ; d. Aug. 14, 1869. Oakland, Cal.
ALICE, born May 14, 1864, died Aug. 18, 1869 at Oakland, Cal.

27 Children of **George Carleton**, son of James Bowdoin. Dexter,
Mich.
CLARA, born 1867.

27 Children of **Charles B.**, son of James Bowdoin. Illinois.
CHARLES OTIS, born November, 1875.

27 Children of **James Bridgeman**, son of James Bowdoin. Dexter,
Mich.
ALICE, born 1870.
BENJAMIN FRANKLIN, born 1872.

•••

EIGHTH GENERATION.

28 Children of **Capt. Robert Bruce**, son of Hinsdale. Burlington,Vt.
ROBERT ANDERSON, born August 19, 1861.

28 Children of **Edwin Herbert**, son of Hinsdale. Guelph, Ont.
NELLIE FELICIA, born April 27, 1868.
AMY EMMA, born August 12, 1871.
CLINTON GOODEVE, born July 1, 1874.

APPENDIX.

THE FAMILIES OF DAUGHTERS OF THE ARMS FAMILY.

It was not the intention of the writer to record families that did not bear the name of Arms, but by request the list is added. It is not complete by any means, but it is correct as far as it goes.

FIFTH GENERATION.

9 Children of **Daniel Chapin** and **Joanna Arms**, daughter of William 3d.

REV. WILLIAM A., married Lucy Curtis.

DWIGHT. Newport, N. II.

DAVID. Newport, N. II.

HORACE. Idiot.

JASON. Graduated at Amherst College ; home missionary. Newport.

FREDERICK. Newport, N. II.

ELIZA. Married Moses Haven.

PHILEMANA. Married R. Bascom.

ANNA. Married Mr. Allis.

9 Children of **Rev. Jacob Havens** and **Asenath Arms**, daughter of William 3d.

MOSES B., died 1873 ; married Eliza Chapin. Plainfield, N. II.

HANNAH, married Sim Wheeler. Newport, N. II.

23 MIRANDA, b. 1799 ; m. William Arms, 5th, (p. 14). Sherbrooke, C. E.

9 Children of **Amos Fisher** and **Huldah Arms**, daughter of William 3d.

AUGUSTUS.

NATHANIEL.

THEODORE.

10 Children of **Samuel Wells** and **Esther Arms**, daughter of Eliakim.

EBENEZER, born August 1, 1795 ; died July 25, 1803.

36 AUGUSTUS, born January 7, 1798, died January 4, 1861 ; married Marinda Arms, (page 13) daughter of Henry. Deerfield.

GEORGE, b. June 23, 1800; m. Sophronia Reed. Bernardstown, Mass.

WILLIAM, born April 2, 1803 ; died October 23, 1816. Deerfield.

24 JANE, born April 6, 1809, died April 2, 1877 : married Seneca Arms, (page 15) son of William 4th, Nov. 6, 1833. Troy, N. Y.

10 Children of **Judah Wright** and **Charlotte Arms,** d. Eliakim.
ELI, died 1867. Deerfield. SOPHIA and REUBEN. Deerfield.

10 Children of **Elijah Sanderson** and **Abigail Arms,** d. Eliakim.
DWIGHT, AUSTIN, MARY, ESTHER, WILLIAM and GEORGE.

SIXTH GENERATION.

11 **David Horton** and **Lucinda Arms,** daughter of Josiah, had
THREE children.

11 **Daniel Goodnow** and **Cynthia Arms,** daughter of Josiah, had
FOUR children.

11 **William Goodnow** and **Sybil Arms,** daughter of Josiah, had
ISAAC, JOTHAM, WILLIAM, MARY, ANN, and EMILINE LUCINDA.
By her second husband, SOLOMON WHITNEY, had ANN, who married
Stephen French, Orange, Mass., and SOLOMON.

11 Children of **Joshua Pratt** and **Martha Arms,** d'r of Aaron.
LUCY TYLER, born March 15, 1826 ; died August 1, 1826.
AARON, born May 3, 1827 ; died May 3, 1827.
SOPHIA, born June 17, 1828 ; died October 20, 1850.
MARTHA, born September 23, 1830.
JAMES C., born June 25, 1835.
ELIZA H., born March 11, 1836.
LUCY TYLER, born November 10, 1839 ; died August 16, 1841.

12 Children of **Rev. William Goodell,** and **Mary Arms,**
daughter of Ebenezer, Jr.
EBENEZER ARMS.
MARY, married Dr. Shaw. Ripon, Wis.

12 Children of **Gen. Thos. D. Gilbert** and **Harriet Arms,**
daughter of Ebenezer, Jr.
THOS. D. JR., FRANCIS B., HARRIET, SUSAN, MARY, and MARTHA,
all of Grand Rapids, Mich.

12 Children of **Eurotas Hastings** and **Evoe Arms,** daughter of
Ebenezer, Jr.
WILLIAM B.
FRANCES, married Dr. Wyckoff. Buffalo, N. Y.

12 Children of **Wm. A. Van Vranken** and **Sophia Arms,**
daughter of Ebenezer, Jr.
MARY. Interior Department, Washington, D. C.

12 Children of **Henry D. Chapman** and **Maria Arms,** d. Daniel.
FOSTER M., ORVILLE, VOLNEY, DANIEL, and ANOTHER, who is dead.

13 Children of **Augustus Wells** and **Marinda Arms,** d'r Henry.
SAMUEL. Deerfield, Mass.
AMELIA, married John Stebbins. Deerfield, Mass.

14 Children of **Rev. Samuel Adsit** and **Jane Maria Arms,** daughter of Abner.

FRANK MARIA, born Nov. 14, 1840, married George K. Share Aug. 27, 1862. Indianapolis.

MINA, born May 17, 1842, married Jas. O. Woodruff Nov. 21, 1861. Indianapolis, Ind.

MARY ELIZA, born Sept. 6, 1844, died Nov. 11, 1867; married Col. Andrew McCowan, of 1st N. Y. Independent Battery Feb. 25, 1864. Now of Louisville, Ky.

CHARLES S., born March 17, 1848. Indianapolis, Ind.

SARAH ELIZABETH, born March 25, 1850, married Col. Fred. W. Clemons Nov. 3, 1869. Palmyra, N. Y.

HENRY BLAINS, born Aug. 11, 1852. Silverton, Col.

14 Children of **Rev. George Plumer** and **Elizabeth Hayden Arms,** daughter of Abner.

CARRIE, born 1859.

14 Children of **Theodore Hale** and **Eliza Hays Arms,** daughter of Abner.

FREDERICK, born 1863.

16 Children of **Col. Jon. P. Miller** and **Sarah Arms,** daughter of Jonathan, Jr.

SARAH, married Abijah Keith. Chicago, Ill.

17 Children of **Henry Hitchcock** and **Martha Arms,** daughter of Pliny.

WILLIAM HENRY, b. Dec. 14, 1842, d. Aug. 25, 1858. Galesburg, Ill.

GEORGE KIMBERLY, b. Jan. 27, 1851, d. Aug. 21, 1851. Galesburg.

MARTHA ARMS, born Oct. 14, 1857. Galesburg, Ill.

17 Children of **George Herbert** and **Theresa T. Arms,** daughter of Pliny.

MARY L., b. April 5, 1841, m. Rev. Henry Huntington Dec. 8, 1870.

THERESA A., born Jan. 18, 1852, married Carrol Gaytes, June 30, 1870. Riverside, Ill.

17 Children of **Wm. Abel** and **Jerusha Smith Arms,** daughter of Eliakim, Jr.

· ELIZA MIRANDA, married Samuel Richards. Elizabeth, N. J.

CALVIN. Goshen, Mass.

CHARLES. Goshen, Mass.

17 Children of **Levi Williams** and **Harriet Arms,** d. Eliakim, Jr.

LEONARD A., born 1821, died Jan. 22, 1866. Albany, N. Y.

JAMES B. Texas.

HARRIET MARIA, died Oct. 11, 1845; m. N. Pike. Albany, N. Y.

GEORGE WEEKS. Albany, N. Y.

17 Children of **Levi Cook** and **Eliza B. Arms,** d'r of Eliakim, Jr.
RALPH LEONARD, married Julia Tivett.
CHARLES ARMS, died ——
CHARLES ARMS, married Sarah Blount.
FRANCES EMMA, born July 14, 1834.

17 Children of **Cyrus Carleton** and **Maria Arms,** d'r Eliakim, Jr.
GEORGE W., born Jan. 16, 1832. Publisher. New York.
CYRUS, born Jan. 1, 1830.
CHARLES ARMS, born May 27, 1836. Capt. U. S. Vols.

SEVENTH GENERATION.

18 Children of **Oliver Mattoon** and **Charlotte Arms,** daughter
of Dr. Willard.
EDWIN, WILLARD and SARAH, all dead.

18 Children of **Edward Wright** and **Susan E. Arms,** daughter
of Dr. Willard. West Haven, Conn.
WILLISTON STEBBINS, born April 15, 1844, married Ella A. Chester,
July 15, 1868.

18 Children of **Joseph Miller** and **Sophia Arms,** daughter of
William. Dummerstown, Vt.
ARMS, ADEN and ANSEL.

18 Children of **Alfred S. Brown** and **Mary Arms,** daughter of
William. Guilford, Vt.
TWO CHILDREN.

19 Children of **Curtis Freeman** and **Cynthia Arms,** d'r. Daniel.
HANNAH, MARY, EZRA, NELSON, ANN, LAURA and JULIA.

19 Children of **John Holden** and **Lucy Arms,** daughter of Daniel.
AVIS, MARY, SOPHIA, EDWIN, born May 7, 1837 ; MELISSA, born
May 7, 1840 ; ELVIRA, VICTORY and RALPH.

19 Children of **John Avery** and **Sophia Arms,** d'r of Daniel.
MARY JANE, WILLIAM HENRY, MARTHA, LUCINDA, CHARLES, LUCY.

19 Children of **Windsor Goddard** and **Mary Arms,** d. Daniel.
DANIEL, MARY, ELISHA, CYNTHIA, MARTHA, WILLARD, ANNIE and
HATTIE.

19 Children of **Luther Blunt** and **Martha Arms,** d'r of Daniel.
SARAH, EMMA, AGNES, and LUTHER, JR.

20 Children of **Otis Bigelow** and **Mary Raymond Arms,**
daughter of Roger N. Washington, D. C.
MARY ARMS, born April 10, 1869.

20 Children of **Thomas F. Payne** and **Lucetta Arms,** daughter
of Orin. Wabash, Ind.
EDWARD F., born Aug. 22, 1853.
BASCOM O., born Dec. 1, 1855.
DEWITT C., born Sept. 23, 1857.
OSSIAN A., born Jan. 12, 1860, died April 12, 1863.
FRANK C., born July 20, 1862.
ANNIE L., born March 8, 1865.
ALBERT J., born Sept. 23, 1868.
FLETCHER A., born March 26, 1872.
HARMON T., born Nov. 5, 1874.

20 Children of **John Dungan** and **Laura Arms,** daughter of Orin.
Benton Co., Ind.
LUCETTA A., born Aug. 28, 1865.
LILLA M., born Dec. 28, 1867.
MATTIE D., born Aug. 20, 1870.
ORIN A., born Nov. 26, 1873.

20 Children of **Benj. F. Bruck** and **Amanda Arms,** d'r of Orin.
ALICE, born May 20, 1867.
ELIZABETH, born Jan. 22, 1870.

20 Children of **H. W. Timmons** and **Cynthia A. Arms,** d. Orin.
TENNIE C., born Oct. 1, 1873, died Oct. 5, 1873.
CYNTHIA, born Oct. 1, 1873, died Oct. 5, 1873.

20 Children of **Martin Metcalf** and **Julia Ann Arms,** daughter
of Albert. Battle Creek, Mich.
FOSTER MARTIN, born Sept. 26, 1857.
ALBERT BALL, born Sept. 7, 1860.
FANNIE MARIA, born July 6, 1869.

20 Children of **J. H. Anderson** and **Margaret A. Arms,** daughter of Albert. Grand Rapids, Mich.
GRACIE, born July 7, 1867.

20 Children of **Joseph B. Wilder** and **Jane Maria Arms,**
daughter of Israel. Youngstown, O.
FREEMAN EDWARD, born Sept. 8, 1845, died July 24, 1855.
MYRON ARMS, born Oct. 19, 1850, died Jan. 29, 1854.
ELISHA LEAVENWORTH, born May 2, 1854.
EMILY ARMS, born June 17, 1858.

21 Children of **Henry Manning** and **Sophia B. Arms,** daughter
of Israel. Youngstown, O.
MARIA LUCRETIA, born May 13, 1856.
ANNIE EDWARDS, born April 20, 1858.
HENRY, born Nov. 14, 1861.

21 Children of **Albert Mann** and **Mattie H. Arms,** daughter of Henry, Jr. Knoxville, Ill.
GEORGE, HARRY A., and WILLIAM HORACE.

21 Children of **Wm. R. Berryhill** and **Emily L. E. Arms,** daughter of Oliver.
JOHN, ELIZABETH, ALICE MAY, and SAMUEL REICE.

21 Children of **R. P. Thompson** and **Sarah G. Arms,** d. Oliver.
EMILY and MINNIE LOUANNA.

21 Children of **Waid Green** and **Fanny M. Arms,** d'r of Oliver.
EVA CAROLINE and NANCY ISABELLA.

22 Children of **Seth Bidwell** and **Nancy E. Arms,** daughter of Israel. Brighton, Mich.
FRANKLIN ELIJAH, ELLA MAY, EMMA ESTELLA, ANNIE BELLE and EDWIN LESLIE.

22 Children of **Elisha A. Calkins** and **Eleanor P. Arms,** daughter of Israel. South Lyon, Mich.
CAROLINE and ELEAZER ELLIS.

22 Children of **Joshua Harker** and **Catherine R. Arms,** daughter of Israel. South Lyon, Mich.
WARD WESSON, EDITH MILLIE and CLARENCE PARSONS.

22 Children of **John F. Moseley** and **Eliza Arms,** daughter of Rev. Selah R. Springfield, Mass. TWO DAUGHTERS.

23 Children of **Jas. G. Milligan** and **Mary E. Arms,** daughter of Dr. William. SIX CHILDREN, three of them now dead.

23 Children of **Luman P. Parker** and **Emily P. Arms,** daughter of Dr. William. THREE CHILDREN.

23 Children of **Samuel Tuck** and **Adeline A. Arms,** daughter of William 5th. Sherbrooke, C. E.
MALCOLM, died in Memphis, Tenn.
THOMAS, married Lizzie Sanborn. Sherbrooke, C. E.

23 Children of **John McNickle** and **Adelia Arms,** daughter of William 5th. Sherbrooke, C. E.
JOHN, GEORGE and JESSIE H.

23 Children of **Lemuel Farwell** and **Calista Arms,** daughter of William 5th. Sherbrooke, C. E.
WILLIAM A. and ALBERT.

23 Children of **Luther P. Fisher** and **Catherine B. Arms,** daughter of Rev. Hiram P., D. D. Oakland, Cal.
WILLIAM, LUCY and GRACIE.

23 Children of **E. A. Berry** and **Lucy Ann Arms,** daughter of Rev. Hiram P., D. D. Terre Haute, Ind.
JOHN A.

24 Children of **Rev. Wm. B. Clarke** and **Sarah Jane Arms**,
daughter of Rev. Hiram P., D. D.
HELEN McGREGOR and JANE BAKER.

24 Children of **Rev. Wm. Howell Taylor** and **Jennie E. Arms**,
daughter of Seneca.
JENNIE LOUISE, born August 24, 1860.
MATTIE ARMS, born December 14, 1861 ; died July 31, 1862.

24 Children of **Chas. K. Wallace** and **Mattie H. Arms**, daughter of Seneca. Brooklyn, N. Y.
WALTER THOMAS, born October 23, 1866.
FLORENCE KEEP, born February 16, 1868.

25 Children of **L. H. Fellows** and **Elizabeth R. Arms**, daughter of Dennis. Deerfield.
JANETTE E., born February 8, 1847.
GEORGE P., born February 22, 1851.

26 Children of **Jos. De Golyer** and **Antoinette Arms**, daughter of Walter. Troy, N. Y.
JOS. B. DEGOLYER, JR.
LILLIAS ADELAIDE, married George C. Baldwin, Jr. Troy, N. Y.

26 Children of **Henry Foster** and **Henrietta Arms**, daughter of Sylvester.
CAROLINE.

26 Children of **Rev. W. T. Morrison** and **Mary E. Arms**,
daughter of Dr. Stillman E.
MARY MAGGIE, GRACE LOUISA, CLARA and WILLIAM T.

26 Children of **Rev. Albert Zabriskie** and **Augusta L. Arms**,
daughter of Dr. Stillman E.
ALBERT and JANE BLANVELT.

26 Children of **Jacob E. Parsons** and **Maria Arms**, daughter of Noadiah L. Yonkers, N. Y.
CARLTON WARD, born November 17, 1854.
WALTER FIELD, born June 2, 1857.
BELLE ARMS, born July 11, 1859.
SOPHIA BALLOU, born August 9, 1861.
BESSIE GREEN, born July 27, 1869.
DUDLEY EVERKEN, born August 6, 1871.

26 Children of **G. Dudley Van Vliet** and **Henrietta Arms**,
daughter of Noadiah L. Albany, N. Y. FIVE CHILDREN.

26 Children of **Edwin B. Hosmer** and **Abby L. Arms**, daughter of Rev. Josiah L. Woodstock, Conn.
ALICE LILLIAN, born August 14, 1864.
ALBERT EDWIN, born April 29, 1871.

6

EIGHTH GENERATION.

28 Children of **Clark Crawford** and **Amelia G. Arms,** daughter of William A. Pontiac, Mich.

WILLIE, born April 6, 1871.

29 Children of **Almon Higgins** and **Tisgah Arms,** daughter of Ralph. South Granby, P. Q.

FRED CLINTON, born Nov. 23, 1875.

29 Children of **John Shelder** and **Ellen L. Arms,** daughter of George A. Greenfield, Mass.

GEORGE ARMS, born July 16, 1872.
FANNIE BELLE, born June 1, 1875.

30 Children of **Henry Wick** and **Mary Arms,** daughter of Myron Israel. Youngstown, O.

HUGH B., born Aug. 28, 1870.
FLORENCE, born Aug. 9, 1872.

FAMILIES THAT BEAR THE NAME OF ARMS,

But Cannot be Traced to the Regular Line of Descendants from the Original William Arms.

THOMAS PERKINS, a native of London, Eng., deserted from an English man-of war, and landed at Boston, 1765. To avoid re-capture he assumed the name of Arms. Married Patty Rhodes in Massachusetts. Afterward moved to Clarendon, Vt., then to Swanton, Vt., and finally settled in St. Armand, P. Q.

Children of **Thomas Perkins,** changed to Arms.

CHARLES. Left a family of several children in Chittenden Co., Vt.

THOMAS, married Martha - —.

WILLIAM, born June 6, 1786 ; married Abigail Woodworth. Lived and died at St. Armand, P. Q.

JOHN. Cattaraugus Co., N. Y.

RICHARD. Went West.

REUBEN. Went West.

POLLY.

PATIENCE.

Children of **William,** one of the above sons of Thomas.

SELLY LEMIRA, born January 15, 1811 ; now dead. Sutton, P. Q.

NAHUM, born February 27, 1814. Otsego, Mich.

PRUELLA DIADAMIA, born February 12, 1816. St. Armand, P. Q.

WILLIAM GARDNER, born March 29, 1818. Berkshire, Vt.

JOHN RILEY, born April 2, 1820. St. Armand, P. Q.

REV. ARNOLD LUTHER, born November 11, 1822. St. Armand, P. Q.

REV. GEORGE WASHINGTON, born November 29, 1824. Swanton, Vt.

MOREY DANIEL, born March 2, 1827. St. Armand, P. Q.

Children of **William Gardner,** son of above William.

BYRON D., born 1849. Boston, Mass.

LOU A., born May 3, 1851.

FERNANDO CORTES, born May 11, 1853.

CHARLES FREMONT, born October 19, 1857.

Capt. GEORGE A. ARMS, of Washington, D. C., is not known to belong to the regular line.

There is another family in Pennsylvania—the name of the original one was either George or Thomas, it is not known which. He settled in Pennsylvania before the revolutionary war.

SECOND GENERATION.

Children of **George** or **Thomas,** near Douglasville, Berks Co., Pa.

GEORGE, born about 1780, died 1832 ; married Julia Wells, who died in June, 1873. Reading, Pa.

HENRY, b. about 1790 ; m. Mary Wells, who d. 1868.   Douglasville, Pa.

JACOB. died 1846, and his wife two years later.

ABRAM,   JOHN,   ELIZABETH,   CATHERINE.

JOHN had a large family.

THIRD GENERATION.

Children of **George,** son of George or Thomas.   Reading, Pa.

JOHN, born July 28, 1812 ; married Julia Ann ——

SUSANNA, born November 5, 1814.

SAMUEL WELLS, born Nov. 5, 1816, died February 13, 1872 ; married Maria Annetta Hoffman, December 1, 1844.

CHARLES AUGUSTUS WELLS, born July 14, 1819 ; married —— Nice. Danville, Pa.

EDMOND W., born March 31, 1821.

CATHERINE, born August 23, 1823.

GEORGE, JR., born October 1, 1826.

SARAH A., born January 24, 1828.

Children of **Jacob,** son of George or Thomas.

SAMUEL ; JOHN, who went to Buffalo in 1840, not heard of since, and Two other sons and three daughters.

FOURTH GENERATION.

Children of **John,** son of George.

WILLIAM, JOHN, and MARY J.

Children of **Samuel Wells,** son of George.

ZACHARY T., born July 25, 1846.

MIRANDA, born February 10, 1848 ; married Henry Snyder, January, 1876 ; has one child, born January, 1877.

GEORGE H., born July 31, 1849.

SAMUEL W., JR., born September 18, 1850 ; married Emma Heller, December 28, 1871.

EMMA M., born April 26, 1852 ; married J. Sechler, August, 1872.

JOHN H., born August 12, 1853.   Abington, Ill.

ELLA, born January 29, 1855 ; m. Louise Eberly, November 5, 1873. Shamokin, Pa.

JULIA A., born March 14, 1857.

AUGUSTUS H., born December 28, 1858.

MARY C., born Oct. 15, 1860.
NORMAN R., born Oct. 24, 1861.
ANNA, born Aug. 13, 1864.
FRANCIS E. C., born May 4, 1866.
WILLIAM, born Dec. 12, 1867.

Children of **C. Augustus W.**, son of George. Danville, Pa.
EMMA J., born January 6, 1847, died July, 1847.
REV. AUGUSTUS N., born August 5, 1848. Principal of school for boys.
Andalusia, Pa.
MARY H., born Nov. 9, 1850, married W. H. Kahler ; has one daughter.
GEORGE W., born March 25, 1852, married A. M. Childs.
LAURA C., born Nov. 10, 1854, married Edwin C. Persel.
CLARA R., born Feb. 4, 1857, married K. Persel.
CHARLES C., born July 26, 1858.

FIFTH GENERATION.

Children of **Samuel W., Jr.**, son of Samuel Wells.
WALTER LEMONT, born Oct. 23, 1873.

Children of **J. Sechler** and **Emma M. Arms**, daughter of Samuel
Wells.
EVA, born 1873.
OLIVE, born February, 1874, died July, 1875.
JACOB EDWARD, born May 8, 1876.

Children of **Louis Eberly** and **Ella Arms**, daughter of Samuel W.
AUGUSTUS JOHN, born October, 1876.

Josiah Haddock, who married **Lydia Arms**, (p. 10,) daughter of
Thomas, had a son, a teacher of elocution, who called himself
Arms, but it is not known that he left a family.

Christopher Arms, of Shelburne Falls, probably belongs to the
regular line, but cannot be placed. He had a son,
LORENZO JOINER, born April 1, 1811, died October 15, 1820 ; married
Sarah Jane Grover Oct. 9, 1836, and lived in Grand Rapids, Mich.

Children of **Lorenzo Joiner**, son of Christopher.
SALMON G., born April 5, 1838, died Sept. 1850.
CLARISSA JANE, born March 2, 1840, died January, 1848.
ADELINE, born Oct. 22, 1842, died 1842.
LUCY M., born Dec. 8, 1843 ; m. Wm. R. Story. Pine Grove, Mich.
CHRISTOPHER, born April 7, 1847 ; m. Louisa Perry. Bangor, Mich.
ROSANA, born March 13, 1849, died December, 1849.
ELIZA JANE, born March 17, 1851, married Enos Tyler.

INDEX TO SONS.

INDEX TO DAUGHTERS.